The Prentice Hall Writer's Guide to Research and Documentation

Sixth Edition

KIRK G. RASMUSSEN
Utah Valley State College

PEARSON

Prentice
Hall

UPPER SADDLE RIVER, NEW JERSEY 07458

© 2004, 2001, 1999, 1997 by PEARSON EDUCATION, INC.
Upper Saddle River, New Jersey 07458

10 9 8 7 6 5 4 3

ISBN 0-13-177997-4

Printed in the United States of America

Contents

1
Using Sources

Locating potential sources for a research project is one thing; deciding which ones to include, where to use them, and how to incorporate them is something else. Some writers begin making use of their sources in early exploratory drafts, perhaps by trying out a significant quotation to see how it brings a paragraph into focus. Others prefer to sift and arrange all of their note cards in neat stacks before making any decisions about what to include in their papers. No matter how you begin writing with sources, at some point you will need to incorporate them smoothly, effectively, and correctly into your paper.

1 Controlling Your Sources

Once you've conducted some research and are ready to begin planning the draft of your paper, you need to decide which sources you will use and how you will use them. You can't make this decision based on how much time you spent finding and analyzing each source; you have to decide according to how useful a source is for answering your research question. You need, that is, to control your sources rather than letting them control you.

Real research about real questions is vital and dynamic. It is always changing. Just as you can't expect your first working thesis to be your final thesis, you can't expect to know in advance which sources are going to prove most fruitful. And don't think you can't collect more information once you start drafting. At each step in the process you will see your research question and answer more clearly, so the research you conduct as you write may be the most useful of all. Similarly, and perhaps especially when you engage in field research, you will gain an increased sense of your audience as your research progresses, which can pay off in more reader-oriented writing.

2 Organizing Your Sources

One of the best strategies for maintaining personal control of your research paper is to make an outline first and then organize your notes accordingly. CAUTION: If you organize your notes in a logical sequence and then write an outline based on that sequence you'll be tempted to find a place for every note and to gloss over areas where you haven't done enough research.

Outline your research conclusions

If you *outline* your research conclusions first, you'll let the logical flow of ideas create the blueprint for your paper. Your outline will change as your ideas continue to develop, so don't get too locked into your early outline. If you can't outline before you write, then be sure to begin writing—if only by drafting a "topic sentence" outline to start major sections—before you arrange your note cards.

Organize your supporting evidence

Once you have outlined or begun drafting and have a good sense of the shape of your paper, **organize** your notes. Arrange the note cards so that they correspond to your outline, and put bibliographic cards in alphabetical order by the author's last name. Integrate field research notes as best you can, depending on their format. Finally, go back to your outline and annotate it to indicate which source goes where. By doing this, you can see if there are any ideas that need more research.

3 Synthesizing Information from Sources

As you prepare to draft, you need to assess all the information you have found and decide which sources are useful. Read your notes critically to evaluate each source, and **synthesize** the material into a new, coherent whole.

Synthesizing material involves looking for connections among different pieces of information and formulating ideas about what these connections mean. The connections may be similar statements made by several sources, or contradictions between two sources. Try to reach some conclusions on your own that extend beyond the information in front of you, then use those conclusions to form the goals for your paper.

Next decide how you will use your source information; base your decisions on your goals for the paper and not on the format of your research notes. Papers written in an effort "to get everything in" are source-driven and all too often read like patch jobs of quotations loosely strung together. Your goal should be to remain the director of the research production, your ideas on center stage and your sources the supporting cast. By synthesizing your information into a unique presentation, you remain at center stage.

Also, keep in mind that referring more than two or three times to a single source—unless it is itself the focus of your paper—undercuts your credibility and suggests overreliance on a single point of view. On the other hand, using synthesis to show how ideas from different sources relate to each other as well as how they relate to your own stance greatly improves the coherence of your essay. If you find yourself referring largely to one source—and therefore one point of view—make sure that you have sufficient references to add other points of view to your paper.

4 Integrating Information from Sources

Once you know which sources you want to use, you still have to decide how the ideas from these sources will appear in your paper. The notes you made during your research may be in many forms. For some sources, you will have copied down direct quotations; for others you will have paraphrased or summarized important information. For some field sources you may have made extensive notes on background information, such as your interview subject's appearance. Simply because you've quoted or paraphrased a particular source in your notes, however, doesn't mean you have to use a quotation or paraphrase from this source in your paper. Make decisions about how to use sources based on your goals, not on the format of your research notes.

At this point, it might be helpful for you to consider our suggestion that taking notes in your own words can pay major dividends in your research-based writing. Of major importance, of course, is the fact that drafting directly from quotations leads to a source-controlled essay—and frequently to a shortage of connecting information between ideas. Taking notes in your own words also helps your comprehension of the ideas and arguments you've read. It encourages you mentally to digest material rather than simply copying, and it makes your rereading of the notes more meaningful. For these and other reasons, practices such as photocopying large chunks of material—or downloading it via computer—are no substitute for the note-*writing* portion of your research work. Moreover, whether you quote, paraphrase, or summarize, you must acknowledge your source through documentation. Different disciplines have different conventions for documentation. The examples in this chapter use the documentation style of the Modern Language Association (MLA), the style preferred in the languages and literature field.

Quoting effectively

Direct quotation provides strong evidence and can add both life and authenticity to your paper.

To quote, you must use an author's or speaker's exact words. Slight changes in wording are permitted in certain cases (see the next section), but these changes must be clearly marked. Although you can't change what a source says, you do have control over how much of it you use. Too much quotation can imply that you have little to say for yourself. Use only as long a quotation as you need to make your point. Remember that quotations should be used to support your points, not to say them for you.

Shortening quotations

Long quotations slow readers down and often have the unintended effect of inviting them to skip over the quoted material. Unless the source quoted is itself the topic of the paper (as in a literary interpretation), limit brief quotations to no more than two per page and long quotations to no more than one every three pages.

Be sure that when you shorten a quotation, you have not changed its meaning. If you omit words within quotations for the sake of brevity, you must indicate that you have done so by using ellipsis points. Any changes or additions must be indicated with brackets.

When to Quote

Direct quotations should be reserved for cases in which you cannot express the ideas better yourself. Use quotations when the original words are especially precise, clear, powerful, or vivid.

- **Precise.** Use quotations when the words are important in themselves or when the author makes fine but important distinctions.

   Government, even in its best state, is but a necessary evil; in its worst state, an intolerable one.
   THOMAS PAINE

- **Clear.** Use quotations when the author's ideas are complex and difficult to paraphrase.

   Paragraphs tell readers how writers want to be read.
   WILLIAM BLAKE

- **Powerful.** Use quotations when the words are especially authoritative and memorable.

   You shall know the truth, and the truth shall make you free.
   ABRAHAM LINCOLN

- **Vivid.** Use quotations when the language is lively and colorful, when it reveals something of the author's or speaker's character.

   Writing. I'm more involved in it, but not as attached.
   KAREN, A STUDENT

ORIGINAL

The human communication environment has acquired biological complexity and planetary scale, but there are no scientists or activists monitoring it, theorizing about its health, or mounting campaigns to protect is resilience. Perhaps it's too new, too large to view as a whole, or too containing—we swim in a sea of information, in poet Gary Snyder's phrase. All the more reason to worry. New things have nastier surprises, big things are hard to change, and containing things are inescapable.

Stewart Brand, *The Media Lab*

INACCURATE QUOTATION

In *The Media Lab*, Stewart Brand describes the control that is exerted by watchdog agencies over modern telecommunications: "The human communication environment has . . . activists monitoring it, theorizing about its health . . ." (258).
By omitting certain words, the writer has changed the meaning of the original source.

ACCURATE QUOTATION

In *The Media Lab*, Stewart Brand notes that we have done little to monitor the growth of telecommunications. Modern communication technology may seem overwhelmingly new, big, and encompassing, but these are reasons for more vigilance, not less: "New things have nastier surprises, big things are hard to change, and containing things are inescapable" (258).

Integrating quotations into your paper

Direct quotations will be most effective when you integrate them smoothly into the flow of your paper. You can do this by providing an explanatory "tag" or by giving one or more sentences of explanation. But allow the quote to do its work. Don't explain the quote in your own words (why quote if you're going to restate the ideas?). Readers should be able to follow your meaning easily and to see the relevance of the quotation immediately.

Using embedded or block format. Brief quotations should be embedded in the main body of your paper and enclosed in quotation marks. According to MLA style guidelines, a brief quotation consists of four or fewer typed lines. NOTE: If you are using a different style manual, be sure to check its requirements. *The Chicago Manual of Style*, for instance, raises the number of lines to eight to ten and the *Publication Manual of the American Psychological Association* specifies 40 or more words for the block format to be used.

```
Photo editor Tom Brennan took ten minutes to sort
through my images and then told me, "Most photography
editors wouldn't take more than two minutes to look at
a portfolio."
```

Longer quotations should be set off in block format. Begin a new line, indent one inch or ten spaces (for MLA), and do not use quotation marks.

```
Katie Kelly focuses on Americans' peculiarly negative
chauvinism, in this case, the chauvinism of New York
residents:
        New Yorkers are a provincial lot. They wear
        their city's accomplishments like blue ribbons.
```

> To anyone who will listen they boast of leading
> the world in everything from Mafia murders to
> porno movie houses. (89)

Ellipses. Sometimes you may omit words from a quotation. In such cases, you have to alert the reader to the fact that you have left out a portion of the author's original passage. You do this by inserting ellipses. (**Note:** The 2003, 6th Edition of the <u>MLA Handbook for Writers of Research Papers</u> *no longer* requires the ellipsis marks to be surrounded by square brackets.)

Katie Kelly focuses on Americans' peculiarly negative chauvinism, in this case, the chauvinism of New York residents:

> New Yorkers . . . wear their city's accomplishments
> like blue ribbons. To anyone who will listen they
> boast of leading the world in everything form
> Mafia murders to porno movie houses. (89)

If Ellipses appear in the work you are quoting, you should put brackets around your ellipses to distinguish them from those used by the author (for MLA). The presence of square brackets signals that *you* have omitted words, *not* the author of the original passage.

Introducing quotations. Introduce all quoted material so that readers know who is speaking, what the quotation refers to, and where it is from. If the author or speaker is well-known, it is especially useful to mention his or her name in an introductory signal phrase.

Henry David Thoreau asserts in *Walden*, "The mass of men lead lives of quiet desperation" (5).

If your paper focuses on written works, you can introduce a quotation with the title rather than the author's name, as long as the reference is clear.

There are certain **signal phrases** to tell the reader that the words or ideas that follow come from another source. Choose a signal phrase that reflects the source's intentions, and to avoid monotony, vary the placement of the signal phrases you use.

Walden sets forth one individual's antidote against the "lives of quiet desperation" led by the working class in mid-nineteenth-century America (Thoreau 5).

If neither the author nor the title of a written source is well known (or the speaker in a field source), introduce the quotation with a brief explanation to give your readers some context.

Verbs Used in Signal Phrases

The verb you choose for a signal phrase should accurately reflect the intention of the source.

acknowledges	concedes	illustrates	reports
admits	concludes	implies	reveals
agrees	declares	insists	says
argues	denies	maintains	shows
asserts	emphasizes	notes	states
believes	endorses	observes	suggests
claims	finds	points out	thinks
comments	grants	refutes	writes

Mary Catherine Bateson, daughter of anthropologist Margaret Mead, has become, in her own right, a student of modern civilization. In *Composing a Life* she writes, "The twentieth century has been called the century of the refugee because of the vast numbers of people uprooted by war and politics from their homes" (8).

Explaining and clarifying quotations. Sometimes you will need to explain a quotation in order to clarify why it's relevant and what it means in the context of your discussion.

In *A Sand County Almanac*, Aldo Leopold invites modern urban readers to confront what they lose by living in the city: "There are two spiritual dangers in not owning a farm. One is the danger of supposing that breakfast comes from the grocery, and the other that heat comes from the furnace" (6). Leopold sees city-dwellers as self-centered children, blissfully but dangerously unaware of how their basic needs are met.

You may also need to clarify what a word or reference means. Do this by using square brackets.

Adjusting grammar when using quotations. A passage containing a quotation must follow all the rules of grammatical sentence structure: tenses should be consistent, verbs and subjects should agree, and so on. If the form of the quotation doesn't quite fit the grammar of your own sentences, you can either quote less of the original source, change your sentences, or make a slight alteration in the quotation. Use this last option sparingly, and always indicate any changes with brackets.

UNCLEAR

In *Sand County Almanac*, Aldo Leopold follows various animals, including a skunk and a rabbit, through fresh snow. He wonders, "What got him out of bed?" (5)

CLEAR

In *Sand County Almanac*, Aldo Leopold follows various animals, including a skunk and a rabbit, through fresh snow. He wonders, "What got [the skunk] out of bed?" (5).

GRAMMATICALLY INCOMPATIBLE

If Thoreau believed, as he wrote in *Walden* in the 1850s, "The mass of men lead lives of quiet desperation" (5), then what would he say of the masses today?
The verb *lead* in Thoreau's original quotation is present tense, but the sentence might call for the past tense form *led*.

GRAMMATICALLY COMPATIBLE

If Thoreau believed, as he wrote in *Walden* in the 1850s, that the masses led "lives of quiet desperation" (5), then what would he say of the masses today?

GRAMMATICALLY COMPATIBLE

In the nineteenth century, Thoreau stated, "The Mass of men lead lives of quiet desperation" (*Walden* 5). What would he say of the masses today?

GRAMMATICALLY COMPATIBLE

If Thoreau thought that in his day, the "mass of men [led] lives of quiet desperation" (*Walden* 5), what would he say of the masses today?

Paraphrasing effectively

Although it is generally wise to write as many research notes as possible in your own words, you may have written down or photocopied many quotations instead of taking the time to put an author's or speaker's ideas into your own words.

To **paraphrase**, you restate a source's ideas in your own words. The point of paraphrasing is to make the ideas clearer (both to your readers and to yourself) and to express the ideas in the way that best suits your purpose. In paraphrasing, attempt to preserve the intent of the original statement and to fit the paraphrased statement smoothly into the immediate context of your essay.

The best way to make an accurate paraphrase is to stay close to the order and structure of the original passage, to reproduce its emphasis and details in roughly the same number of words. The paraphrase and the original should be approximately the same (or similar) in length. However, don't use the same sentence patterns or vocabulary or you risk inadvertently plagiarizing the source. (See page 10.)

If the original source has used a well-established or technical term for a concept, you do not need to find a synonym for it. If you believe that the original source's exact words are the best possible expressions of some points, you may use brief direct quotations within your paraphrase, as long as you indicate these with quotation marks.

Keep in mind why you are including this source; doing so will help you to decide how to phrase the ideas. Be careful, though, not to introduce your own comments or reflections in the middle of a paraphrase, unless you make it very clear that these are your thoughts, not the original author's or speaker's.

ORIGINAL

The affluent, educated, liberated women of the First World, who can enjoy freedom unavailable to any woman ever before, do not feel as free as they want to. And they can no longer restrict to the subconscious their sense that this lack of freedom has something to do with—with apparently frivolous issues, things that really should not matter. Many are ashamed to admit that such trivial concerns—to do with physical appearance, bodies, faces, hair, clothes—matter so much.

Naomi Wolf, *The Beauty Myth*, 9

INACCURATE PARAPHRASE

In *The Beauty Myth*, Naomi Wolf argues that First-World women, who still have less freedom than they would like to have, restrict to their subconscious those matters having to do with physical appearance—that these things are not really important to them (9).

ACCURATE PARAPHRASE

In *The Beauty Myth*, Wolf asserts that First-World women, despite their affluence, education, and liberation, still do not feel very free. Moreover, many of these women are aware that this lack of freedom is influenced by superficial things having primarily to do with their physical appearance—things which should not matter so much (9).

Summarizing effectively

To **summarize**, you distill a source's words down to the main ideas and state these in your own words. A summary includes only the essentials of the original source, not the supporting details, and is consequently shorter than the original.

Keep in mind that summaries are generalizations and that many generalizations can make your writing vague and tedious. Summaries are most useful for introducing ideas and concepts and for drawing conclusions. You should occasionally supplement summaries with brief direct quotations or evocative details collected through observation to keep readers in touch with the original source.

When to Summarize

As you draft, summarize often so that your paper doesn't turn into a string of undigested quotations.

- **Main points.** Use summary when your readers need to know the main point the original source makes but not the supporting details.
- **Overviews.** Sometimes you may want to devise a few sentences that will effectively support your discussion without going on and on. Use summary to provide an overview or an interesting aside without digressing too far from your paper's focus.
- **Condensation.** You may have taken extensive notes on a particular article or observation only to discover in the course of drafting that you do not need all that detail. Use summary to condense lengthy or rambling notes into a few effective sentences.

Summaries vary in length, and the length of the original source is not necessarily related to the length of the summary you write. Depending on the focus of your paper, you may need to summarize an entire novel in a sentence or two, or you may need to summarize a brief journal article in two or three paragraphs. Remember that the more material you attempt to summarize in a short space, the more you will necessarily generalize and abstract it. Reduce a text as far as you can while still providing all the information your readers need to know. Be careful, though, not to distort the original's meaning.

ORIGINAL

For a long time I never liked to look a chimpanzee straight in the eye—I assumed that, as is the case with most primates, this would be interpreted as a threat or at least as a breach of good manners. Not so. As long as one looks with gentleness, without arrogance, a chimpanzee will understand and may even return the look.

Jane Goodall, *Through a Window 12*

10

INACCURATE SUMMARY

Goodall learned from her experiences with chimpanzees that they react positively to direct looks from humans (12).

ACCURATE SUMMARY

Goodall reports that when humans look directly but gently into chimpanzees' eyes, the chimps are not threatened and may even return the look (12).

5 Understanding and Avoiding Plagiarism

Acknowledging your sources through one of the accepted systematic styles of **documentation** is a service to your sources, your readers, and future scholars. Knowledge in the academic community is cumulative, with one writer's work building on another's. After reading your paper, readers may want to know more about a source you cited, perhaps in order to use it in papers of their own. Correct documentation helps them find the source quickly and easily.

Failure to document your sources is called **plagiarism**. Plagiarism is taking someone's ideas or information and passing them off as your own. The practice of citing sources for "borrowed" ideas or words is both customary and expected in academic writing.

Most plagiarism is not intentional; many writers are simply unaware of the conventional guidelines for indicating that they have borrowed words or ideas from someone else. Nevertheless, it is the writer's responsibility to learn these guidelines and follow them.

Using a documentation style

Each discipline, or area of academic study, has developed its own conventions for documentation, a standardized set of guidelines that continue to evolve as the discipline evolves. The languages and literature disciplines use the style recommended by the Modern Language Association (MLA). Other humanities use a system of endnotes or footnotes. Social sciences use the style recommended by the American Psychological Association (APA). Natural sciences use the style recommended by the Council of Science Editors (CSE) or a related style. Many disciplines in the physical sciences use the Chicago style (CMS) or the American Institute of Physics Style Manual (AIP). You should use the documentation of the discipline for which you are writing; if you are in doubt, ask your instructor.

Basically, you must attribute any idea or wording you use in your writing to the source through which you encountered that idea or those words, *if the material is not original to yourself.* You do not need to document *common knowledge*, that is, information that an educated person can be expected to know—knowledge commonly taught in school or carried in the popular media—or knowledge that can be found in multiple sources (encyclopedias, dictionaries). Examples include the dates of historical events, the names and locations of states and cities, the general laws of science, and so on. However, when you read the work of authors who have specific opinions and interpretations of a piece of common knowledge and you use

Avoiding Plagiarism

- Place all quoted passages in quotation marks and provide source information, even if it is only one phrase.
- Identify the source from which you have paraphrased or summarized ideas, just as you do when you quote directly.
- Give credit for any creative ideas you borrow from an original source. For example, if you use an author's anecdote to illustrate a point, acknowledge it.
- Replace unimportant language with your own, and use different sentence structures when you paraphrase or summarize.
- Acknowledge the source if you borrow any organizational structure or headings from an author. Don't use the same subtopics, for example.
- Put any words or phrases you borrow in quotation marks, especially an author's unique way of saying something.

their opinions or interpretations in your paper, you must give them credit through proper documentation.

It is also important to note that even "nonpublished" ideas or words should be attributed to their sources whenever such documentation is feasible. For example, if you use opinions from a sidewalk poll, conversation, or Internet commentaries or a World Wide Web (WWW) page in your writing, you must cite that original source.

Avoiding plagiarism

If you are not sure what you can take from a source and what you need to cite, ask a tutor or your instructor for help before you turn in your final paper. Also find out if your school has a booklet on avoiding plagiarism.

Most campuses with Online Writing Labs (OWL's) now have information about plagiarism available through Gopher or WWW. Similarly, your campus OWL, if one exists, is also likely to provide an e-mail-based "hot line" for rapid, direct answers to important questions about plagiarism.

The most common incidence of inadvertent plagiarism is a writer's paraphrasing or summarizing a source but staying too close to the wording or sentence structure of the original, sometimes lifting whole phrases without enclosing them in quotation marks. Keep in mind that when you paraphrase or summarize a source, you need to identify the author of those ideas just as if you had quoted directly.

To avoid plagiarism when you paraphrase, use your own words to replace language that is not important to quote exactly; in other words, you are attributing the ideas, but not the exact language, to the source. At the same time, make certain you cite *all* direct quotes, acknowledging that you are borrowing both the ideas *and the words*.

ORIGINAL

The World Wide Web makes world-wide publishing possible to anyone who is able to arrange disk space on a server and has some basic knowledge of how pages are created.

Carol Lea Clark, A Student's Guide to the Internet

PLAGIARIZED PARAPHRASE

World-wide publishing is possible for anyone who has access to server disk-space and who has knowledge of how Web pages are made. (Clark 77).
The above example uses too much language from the original source.

ACCEPTABLE PARAPHRASE

With the basics of Web-page construction and storage space on a network server, Clark tells us, anyone can publish, at least potentially, for audiences around the world.
This example translates source language into the writer's own language.

2

Documenting Sources: MLA Style

The Modern Language Association (MLA) system is the preferred form for documenting research sources when you write about literature or language.

- All sources are briefly documented in the text by an identifying name and page number (generally in parentheses).
- A Works Cited section at the end of the paper lists full publication data for each source cited.
- Additional explanatory information provided by the writer of the paper (but not from external sources) goes in footnotes either at the foot of the page or in a Notes section after the close of the paper.

The MLA system is explained in more detail in the MLA Handbook for Writers of Research Papers, 6th ed. (New York: MLA, 2003).

Directory for MLA Documentation Guidelines

CONVENTIONS FOR IN-TEXT CITATIONS

1. Single work by one or more authors
2. Two or more works by the same author
3. Unknown author
4. Corporate or organizational author
5. Authors with the same last name
6. Works in more than one volume
7. One-page works
8. Quote from an indirect source
9. Literary works
10. More than one work in a citation
11. Works in an anthology or other collection
12. Long quote set off from text
13. Electronic sources

CONVENTIONS FOR ENDNOTES AND FOOTNOTES

CONVENTIONS FOR LIST OF WORKS CITED

Directory for MLA Documentation Guidelines (continued)

DOCUMENTING BOOKS

1. Book by one author
2. Book by two or three authors
3. Book by more than three authors
4. More than one book by the same author
5. Book by a corporation, association, or organization
6. Revised edition of a book
7. Edited book
8. Book with an editor and an author
9. Book in more than one volume
10. One volume of a multi-volume book
11. Translated book
12. Book in a series
13. Reprinted book
14. Introduction, preface, foreword, or afterward in a book
15. Work in an anthology or chapter in an edited collection
16. Two or more works from the same anthology or collection
17. Periodical article reprinted in a collection
18. Article in a reference book
19. Anonymous book
20. Government document
21. Dissertation: unpublished, published
22. A pamphlet
23. A book with missing publication information
24. Titles within titles

DOCUMENTING PERIODICALS

25. Article, story, or poem in a monthly or bimonthly magazine
26. Article, story, or poem in a weekly magazine
27. Article in a daily newspaper
28. Article in a journal paginated by volume
29. Article in a journal paginated by issue
30. Anonymous article
31. Microform or microfiche article
32. Editorial
33. Letter to the editor and reply
34. Review

Directory for MLA Documentation Guidelines (continued)

DOCUMENTING ELECTRONIC SOURCES

35. Book
36. Scholarly project
37. Professional site
38. Personal site
39. Government site
40. Academic home page
41. Course home page
42. Online work of art
43. Online film or film clip
44. Online cartoon
45. Online TV or radio program
46. Article in an online database
47. Article in a journal
48. Article in a magazine
49. Posting to a discussion list
50. CD-ROM database, periodically updated
51. CD-ROM, non-periodical
52. Diskettes
53. Electronic texts
54. An e-mail message
55. Public postings on electronics networks
56. Synchronous communication
57. Work from a library or personal subscription service
58. Software programs
59. Publication on magnetic tape
60. Publication in more than one medium
61. Other online materials with URLs

DOCUMENTING OTHER SOURCES

62. Cartoon
63. Film, videocassette or DVD
64. Personal interview
65. Published or broadcast interview
66. Print advertisement
67. Unpublished lecture, public address, or speech
68. Personal or unpublished letter
69. Published letter
70. Map
71. Performance
72. Audio recording
73. Television or radio broadcast
74. Work of art

The MLA system provides a simple, economic (concise), and thorough way for writers to acknowledge the sources they use in research-based papers. In the MLA system, authors use footnotes and/or endnotes to provide additional, explanatory information, but not to cite information provided by external sources. Whenever possible, the MLA system includes explanatory information in the text itself and limits the use of footnotes or endnotes. Pay careful attention to the practical mechanics of documentation, so that readers can readily identify, understand, and locate your sources.

1 Conventions for In-Text Citations

In-text citations identify ideas and information borrowed from other writers. They also refer readers to the works cited list at the end of the paper, where they can find complete publication information about each original source. The languages and literature are not primarily concerned with *when* something was written; instead, these fields of study focus on writers and the internal qualities of texts. Therefore, in-text citations following the MLA style, feature author names, text titles, and page numbers. MLA style is economical, providing only as much in-text information as readers need in order to locate more complete information in the Works Cited. Following are some examples of how in-text citation works; pages 26–46 for the format of entries in the Works Cited, and pages 47–50 for sample pages using MLA documentation.

To maintain ease of reading, the MLA style prefers parenthetical references (citations) to be as brief and as few as possible; only enough should be used for clarity and accuracy. Usually a source may be acknowledged by naming the author and the specific page number wherein the information may be found, but if you are referring to the entire work the MLA prefers that you incorporate the author's name into the sentence without using parentheses for citing particular portions of the work ("Thomas Jones describes this accessing technique" would be enough if there is only one work by Jones listed on the Works Cited page and you aren't pointing the reader to a particular place in that work).

Citations in-text must clearly identify the sources listed on the Works Cited page. You must give enough information so the reader has no trouble finding the more complete information contained in the Works Cited. Your parenthetical citation mirrors whatever information is used to start the entry on the Works Cited page: author, corporate author's name (which can be shortened or abbreviated if it remains clear, such as IBM instead of International Business Machines), or the title of the work if no author is named. If you have more than one author with the same last name, provide initials to distinguish them. If your source has multiple authors, you must list their last names. If a source has more than three authors, follow the pattern used on the Works Cited page of giving the first author's last name and the "et al." abbreviation, as in (Jones et al. 15—19).

If you are quoting from a source, you must include the specific portions of the source, which means page numbers (the volume number of the work also if it is multi-volumed). In some cases, you may want for additional clarity to include chapter numbers for literary works, act and scene numbers for plays, and line numbers for poems. You can leave out page numbers if, for instance, the source contains articles arranged alphabetically (as in a reference work); if your source doesn't have page numbers, as in an electronic source; or if your source has only one page.

Less useful information, such as abbreviations designating the function of the author (*ed., trans.,* and *comp.*), as in (Jones, ed. 15–19), add nothing of substance to the citation and increase the reader's burden. The key is to <u>simplify</u> the citation—nothing more than must be there, and only there if it must be there.

1. Single work by one or more authors

When you quote, paraphrase, or summarize a source, include in the text of your paper the last name of the source's author, if known, and, in parentheses, the page or pages on which the original information appeared. Do not include the word *page* or the abbreviations *p.* or *pp.* You may mention the author's name in the sentence or put it in parentheses, preceding the page number(s).

    Carol Lea Clark explains the basic necessities for the
    creation of a page on the World Wide Web (77).

    Provided one has certain "basic ingredients," the Web
    offers potential worldwide publication to individuals
    (Clark 77).

Note that a parenthetical reference at the end of a sentence comes before the period. No punctuation is used between the author's last name and the page number(s).

If you cite a work with two or three authors, your in-text parenthetical citation must include all authors' names: (Rombauer and Becker 715), (Child, Bertholle, and Beck 215). For works with more than three authors, you may list all the authors or, to avoid awkwardness, use the first author's name and add "et al." without a comma: (Britton et al. 395). *Et al.* is an abbreviation for the Latin *et alii*, translated "and others."

2. Two or more works by the same author

If your paper has references to two or more works by the same author, you should clearly identify the specific work in your citation. Either mention the title of the work in the text or include a shortened version of the title (usually the first one or two important words) in the parenthetical citation.

    According to Lewis Thomas in <u>Lives of a Cell</u>, many
    bacteria become dangerous only if they manufacture
    exotoxins (76).

According to Lewis Thomas, many bacteria become
dangerous only if they manufacture exotoxins (<u>Lives</u> 76).

Many bacteria become dangerous only if they manufacture
exotoxins (Thomas, <u>Lives</u> 76).

If both the author's name and a shortened version of the title are in a parenthetical citation, a comma separates them, but there is no comma before the page number.

3. Unknown author

When the author of a work you are citing is unknown, use either the complete title in the text or a shortened version of it in the parenthetical citation, along
with the page number.

According to <u>Statistical Abstracts</u>, the literacy rate
for Mexico stood at 75% in 1990, up 4% from census figures
ten years earlier (374).

The literacy rate for Mexico stood at 75% in 1990, up
4% from census figures ten years earlier (<u>Statistical</u> 374).

4. Corporate or organizational author

When no author is listed for a work published by a corporation, organization,
or association, indicate the group's full name in any parenthetical reference:
(Florida League of Women Voters 3). If the name is long, cite it in the sentence and
put only the page number in parentheses.

5. Authors with the same last name

When you cite works by two or more authors with the same last name, include
the first initial of each author's name in the parenthetical citation: (C. Miller 63; S.
Miller 101–4).

6. Works in more than one volume

When your sources are in more than one volume of a multivolume work, indicate the pertinent volume number for each citation. Place the volume number
before the page number and follow it with a colon and one space: (Hill 2: 70). If
your source is in only one volume of a multivolume work, you need not specify the
volume number in the in-text citation, but you should specify it in the Works Cited.

7. One-page works

When you refer to a work in your text that is only one page long, you need not
include the page number in your citation. Author or title identification is sufficient for readers to find the exact page number on the Works Cited list.

8. Quote from an indirect source

When a quotation or any information in your source is originally from another source, use the abbreviation "qtd. in."

    Lester Brown of Worldwatch feels that international
    agricultural production has reached its limit and that
    "we're going to be in trouble on the food front before
    this decade is out" (qtd. in Mann 51).

9. Literary works

In citing literary prose works available in various editions, provide additional information (such as chapter number or scene number) for readers who may be consulting a different edition. Use a semicolon to separate the page number from this additional information: (331; bk. 10, ch. 5). In citing poems, provide only line numbers for reference; include the word "line" or "lines" in the first such reference. Providing information will help your audience find the passages *in any source where those works are reprinted*, which page references alone cannot provide.

    In "The Mother," Gwendolyn Brooks remembers ". . . the
    children you got that you did not get" (line 1); children
    that "never giggled or planned or cried" (30).

Cite verse plays using act, scene, and line numbers, separated by periods: (*Hamlet* 4.4.31–39).

10. More than one work in a citation

To cite more than one work in a parenthetical reference, separate them with semicolons: (Aronson, *Golden Shore* 177; Didion 49-50).

11. Work in an anthology or other collection

When you are quoting from an anthology, a book containing the works of many authors, your in-text citation should name the author of the article, short story, poem, play, or chapter you are quoting, not the editor(s) who compiled the anthology. For example, suppose you quote from Mona Charon's "Much More Nasty Than They Should Be," which appears in an anthology by Donald McQuade and Robert Atwan. Cite Charon's name and the title of her work in the in-text citation; then begin the entry in the Works Cited list with Charon's name. (See section 15 on p. 29 for the Charon entry in the Works Cited list for the quote that follows. Also see section 16 on p. 30 for a refinement of this rule regarding anthology entries in the Works Cited list.)

In "Much More Nasty Than They Should Be," Mona Charon describes censorship as "a defining act of civilization," arguing that "[s]ociety cannot exist without prescribing certain things" (208).

12. Long quote set off from text

For quotes of more than four lines, set off the quote from the text by indentation. Indent the quote one inch or ten spaces from the left margin of the text (not from the paper's edge), double-space, and omit quotation marks. The parenthetical citation follows end punctuation (unlike shorter, integrated quotes) and is not followed by a period.

Fellow author W. Somerset Maugham had this to say about Austen's dialogue:

> No one has ever looked upon Jane Austen as a great stylist. Her spelling was peculiar and her grammar often shaky, but she had a good ear. Her dialogue is probably as natural as dialogue can ever be. To set down on paper speech as it is spoken would be very tedious, and some arrangement of it is necessary. (434)

13. Electronic sources

If an electronic source does not include page numbers, cite just the element that begins the entry on the Works Cited page (author or title). Better yet, incorporate the author's name (or work's title) into the discussion rather than using a parenthetical citation. If your source includes pages or paragraphs in its Works Cited entry, you can designate the particular page or paragraph (Jones, par. 3) (Jones 6).

2 Conventions for Endnotes and Footnotes

In MLA citation style, notes are used primarily to offer comments, explanations, or additional information (especially source-related information) that cannot be smoothly or easily accommodated in the text of the paper. You might use notes also to cite several sources within a single context if a series of *in-text* references might detract from the readability of the text. In general, however, you should omit additional information, outside the "mainstream" of your text, unless it is necessary for clarification or justification.

If you conclude that a note is necessary, insert a raised (superscript) numeral at the reference point in the text; introduce the note itself with a corresponding raised numeral, and indent it. Many word processing programs provide footnote functions, which greatly simplify the entire procedure.

TEXT WITH SUPERSCRIPT

The standard ingredients for guacamole include avocados, lemon juice, onion, tomatoes, coriander, salt, and pepper.[1] Hurtado's poem, however, gives this traditional dish a whole new twist (lines 10-17).

NOTE

[1]For variations see Beard 314, Egerton 197, Eckhardt 92, and Kafka 26. Beard's version, which includes olives and green peppers, is the most unusual.

The references listed in the notes should appear in the Works Cited along with the other sources referred to in your text.

Notes may come at the bottom of the page on which the text reference appears-as footnotes—or be included as endnotes, double—spaced, on a separate page at the end of your paper. Endnote pages should be placed between the text of the paper and the Works Cited, with the title "Note" or "Notes."

3 Conventions for List of Works Cited

All sources mentioned in an academic essay (and other types of formal or professional writing) should be identified on a concluding list of Works Cited. These entries follow specific rules for formatting and punctuation so that the reader can readily find information.

Format. After the final page of the paper, title a separate page "Works Cited," an inch from the top of the page, centered, but not underlined and not in quotation marks. Exception: If you are required to list all the works you have read in researching the topic—not just those to which you have actually referred in your text or notes—you should title this list "Works Consulted" rather than "Works Cited." Number the page, following in sequence from the last page of your paper.

Double-space between the Works Cited title and your first entry. Begin each entry at the left margin, indenting the second and all subsequent lines of each entry five spaces. Double-space both between and within entries (in other words, double-space all lines of the Works Cited list). If the list runs to more than one page, continue numbering pages in sequence but do not repeat the title.

Order of entries. Alphabetize the entries according to authors' last names. If two or more authors have the same last name, alphabetize by first name or initial. For entries by an unknown author, alphabetize according to the first word of the title, excluding an initial *A*, *An*, or *The*.

Format for entries. There are many variations on the following general formats, given the additional information needed to identify various kinds of sources. The following formats are the three most common.

Authors. Authors are listed last name first, followed by a comma and the rest of the name as it appears on the publication. A period follows the full name. If a work has more than one author, list the subsequent names first name first, and separate the names with a comma. When the Works Cited has more than one work by the same author, substitute three hyphens for the author's name after the first entry.

Titles. List the titles and subtitles fully, capitalizing them as in the original. Underline the titles of entire books and periodicals; put quotation marks around the titles of essays, poems, and other works that are part of a larger (entire) work. Put the name of a periodical after a book or article title; no punctuation should follow a journal, magazine, or newspaper title.

Places of publication. For books, always give the city of publication. If several cities are listed on the title or copyright pages, give only the first. If the name of the city alone could be unfamiliar or confusing to your readers, add an abbreviation for the state or country. However, when the name of the state appears in the publisher's name (as in many university presses), you should not add the name of the state (e.g., "Jackson: University of Mississippi Press," *not* "Jackson, MI: University of Mississippi Press"). Finally, use a comma to separate the city from the state or country and a colon to separate the place of publication from the publisher.

Publishers. If the title page indicates that a book is published under an imprint—for example, Arbor House is an imprint of William Morrow—list both imprint and publisher, separated by a hyphen (Arbor-Morrow). For books, use a comma to separate the publisher from the publication date.

Dates and page numbers. For books and periodicals, give only the year of publication. Place a period after the year of publication for a book; place the year of publication for periodicals within parentheses, followed by a colon and a space. For dates of newspapers, use no commas between the elements and put the day before the month (14 June 2002). For magazines and newspapers, place a colon and a space after the date of publication. Separate inclusive page numbers with a hyphen (42–54). Up to 99, use all the digits for the second page numbers, and above 99 list the last two digits only (130–38) unless the full sequence is needed for clarity (198–210). If the page numbers are not consecutive (as in a newspaper), place a plus sign after the final consecutive page (39+, 52–55+). The plus sign represents *all* subsequent pages in the work cited, regardless of how many there are or how they are arranged.

GENERAL FORMAT FOR BOOKS

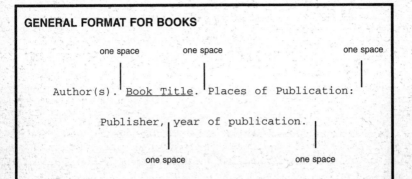

one space   one space   one space

Author(s). <u>Book Title</u>. Places of Publication:

Publisher, year of publication.

one space   one space

GENERAL FORMAT FOR JOURNAL ARTICLES

Author(s). "Author Title." <u>Journal Title</u>

volume number year of publication:

inclusive page numbers.

GENERAL FORMAT FOR MAGAZINE AND NEWSPAPER ARTICLES

Author(s). "Article Title." <u>Publication Title</u> date

of Publication : inclusive page numbers.

Documenting books

1. Book by one author

Benjamin, Jessica. <u>The Bonds of Love: Psychoanalysis,</u>
    <u>Feminism, and the Problem of Domination</u>. New York:
    Prometheus, 1988.

2. Book by two or three authors

Zweigenhaft, Richard L., and G. William Domhoff. <u>Blacks in</u>
    <u>the White Establishment</u>. New Haven: Yale UP, 1991.

Author names after the first are identified first name first, and the final
author's name is preceded by "and."

3. Book by more than three authors

Belenky, Mary Field, et al. <u>Women's Ways of Knowing: The</u>
    <u>Development of Self, Voice, and Mind</u>. New York: Basic,
    1986.

If a work has more than three authors, you may use the Latin abbreviation "et
al." or list all the authors' names in full as they appear on the title page.

4. More than one book by the same author

Nelson, Mariah Burton. <u>Are We Winning Yet?: How Women Are</u>
    <u>Changing Sports and Sports Are Changing Women</u>. New
    York: Basic, 1991.

---. <u>The Stronger Women Get, The More Men Love Football:</u>
    <u>Sexism and the American Culture of Sports</u>. New York:
    Harcourt, 1993.

Selfe, Cynthia L. "Creating a Computer Lab that Composition
    Teachers Can Live with." <u>Collegiate Microcomputer</u> 5
    (1987): 149-58.

Selfe, Cynthia L., and Billie J. Wahlstrom. "An Emerging
    Rhetoric of Collaboration: Computer Collaboration and
    the Composing Process." <u>Collegiate Microcomputer</u> 4
    (1986): 289-96.

If your Works Cited list contains more than one source by the same author or authors, in the second and all additional entries by that author replace the author's name with three hyphens (no spaces) followed by a period. The hyphens represent the exact name of the author in the preceding entry. If a source's author is not identical to that in the preceding entry, list author names in full. Two or more works with the same author are alphabetized according to title; a work by a single author precedes works by that author and one or more collaborators.

5. Book by a corporation, association, or organization

Society of Automotive Engineers. <u>Effects of Aging on Driver Performance</u>. Warrendale, PA: Society of Automatic Engineers, 1988.

Alphabetize by the name of the organization.

6. Revised edition of a book

Peek, Stephen. <u>The Game Inventor's Handbook</u>. 2nd ed. Cincinnati: Betterway, 1993.

For second or any subsequent editions of a book, place the appropriate numerical designation (2nd ed., 3rd ed., etc.) after the name of the editor, translator, or compiler, if there is one. If not, place it after the title.

7. Edited book

Schaefer, Charles E., and Steven E. Reid, eds. <u>Game Play: Therapeutic Use of Childhood Games</u>. New York: Wiley, 1986.

For books with a listed editor or editors but no author, place the name of the editor(s) in the author position, followed by "ed." or "eds."

8. Book with an editor and an author

Hemingway, Ernest. <u>Conversations with Ernest Hemingway</u>. Ed. Matthew J. Bruccoli. Jackson: UP of Mississippi, 1986.

Books with both an editor and an author should be listed with the editor following the title, first name first, preceded by the abbreviation "Ed." This convention holds true whether one or more editors are listed.

9. Book in more than one volume

Waldrep, Tom, ed. <u>Writers on Writing</u>. 2 vols. New York: Random, 1985-88.

The total number of volumes is listed after the title. When separate volumes were published in different years, provide inclusive dates.

10. One volume of a multi-volume book

Waldrep, Tom, ed. <u>Writers on Writing</u>. Vol. 2. New York: Random, 1988.

When each volume of a multivolume set has an individual title, list the volume's full publication information first, followed by series information (number of volumes, dates).

Churchill, Winston S. <u>Triumph and Tragedy</u>. Boston: Houghton, 1953. Vol. 6 of <u>The Second World War</u>. 6 vols. 1948-53.

11. Translated book

Klaeber, Friedrich. <u>Beowulf and the Finnesburg Fragment</u>. Trans. John R. Clark Hall. Rev. ed. London: Allen, 1950.

12. Book in a series

<u>First NASA Workshop on Wiring for Space Applications</u>. NASA Conference Publication. 10145. Washington: National Aeronautics and Space Administration, Office of Management, Scientific and Technical Information Program, 1994.

Immediately after the title, add the series information: the series name, neither underlined nor in quotation marks, and the series number, both followed by periods. Book titles within an underlined title are not underlined.

13. Reprinted book

Evans, Elizabeth E. G. <u>The Abuse of Maternity</u>. 1875. New York: Arno, 1974.

Add the original publication date after the title, then cite the current edition information.

14. Introduction, preface, foreword, or afterword in a book

Gavorse, Joseph. Introduction. <u>The Lives of the Twelve Caesars</u>. By Suetonius. New York: The Book League of America, 1937. Vii-xvi.

Jacobus, Lee A. Preface. <u>Literature: An Introduction to</u>
    <u>Critical Reading</u>. By Jacobus. Upper Saddle River, NJ:
    Prentice Hall, 1996. Xxvii–xxxiii.

Nabokov, Vladimir. Foreword. <u>A Hero of Our Time</u>. By Mihail
    Lermontov. Garden City, NY: Doubleday-Anchor, 1958.
    V–xix.

List the author of the introduction, preface, foreword, or afterword first, followed by the title of the book. Next insert the word "By," followed by the full
name of the author of the whole work if different from the author of the piece, or
the last name only if the same as the author of the shorter piece.

Cooper, Bernard. "The Disproportionate Power of the Small."
    Preface. <u>In Short: A Collection of Brief Creative</u>
    <u>Nonfiction</u>. Eds. Judith Kitchen and Mary Paumier Jones.
    New York: W.W. Norton and Company, 1991. 17–22.

But if the introduction, preface, foreword, or afterword has a title, enclose the
title in quotation marks after the author's name, followed by a period and the word
"Introduction," "Preface," "Foreword," or "Afterword." If the book with this titled
introduction, preface, foreword, or afterword is a work that was edited by someone
else, insert the word "Ed" or "Eds" instead of "By," and then list the name of the
editor or editors.

15. Work in an anthology or chapter in an edited collection

Charen, Mona. "Much More Nasty Than They Should Be."
    <u>Popular Writing in America: The Interaction of Style</u>
    <u>and Audience</u>. 5th ed. Ed. Donald McQuade and Robert
    Atwan. New York: Oxford UP, 1993. 207–8.

Gay, John. <u>The Beggar's Opera. British Dramatists from</u>
    <u>Dryden to Sheridan</u>. Ed. George H. Nettleton and Arthur
    E. Case. Carbondale: Southern Illinois UP, 1975.
    530–65.

Kingston, Maxine Hong. "No Name Woman." 1976. <u>The Blair</u>
    <u>Reader</u>. 2nd ed. Ed. Laurie G. Kirszner and Stephen R.
    Mandell. Upper Saddle River, NJ: Prentice Hall, 1996.
    46–56.

Enclose the title of the work in quotation marks unless it was originally published as a book, in which case it should be underlined. The title of the anthology follows the book title and is underlined. At the end of the entry, provide inclusive page numbers for the selection. For previously published nonscholarly works, you may, as a courtesy to your reader, include the year of original publication after the title of the anthologized work. Follow this date with a period.

16. Two or more works from the same anthology or collection

Kingston, Maxine Hong. "No Name Woman." Kirszner and
     Mandell 46-56.

Kirszner, Laurie G., and Stephen R. Mandell, eds. <u>The Blair</u>
     <u>Reader</u>. 2nd ed. Upper Saddle River, NJ: Prentice Hall,
     1996.

Tannen, Deborah. "Marked Women." Kirszner and Mandell
     362-67.

When citing two or more selections from one anthology, list the anthology separately under the editor's name. Selection entries will then need to include only a shortened cross-reference to the anthology entry, as illustrated above.

17. Periodical article reprinted in a collection

Atwell, Nancie. "Everyone Sits at a Big Desk: Discovering
     Topics for Writing." <u>English Journal</u> 74 (1985): 35-39.
     Rpt. in <u>Rhetoric and Composition: A Sourcebook for</u>
     <u>Teachers and Writers</u>. 3rd ed. Ed. Richard Graves.
     Portsmouth, NH: Boynton/Cook, 1990. 76-83.

Include the full citation for the original periodical publication, followed by "Rpt. in" (Reprinted in) and the book publication information. Provide inclusive page numbers for both sources.

18. Article in a reference book

"Behn, Aphra." <u>The Concise Columbia Encyclopedia</u>. 1983 ed.

"Langella, Frank." <u>International Television and Video</u>
     <u>Almanac</u>. 40th ed. New York: Quigley, 1995.

Miller, Peter L. "The Power of Flight." <u>The Encyclopedia of</u>
     <u>Insects</u>. Ed. Christopher O'Toole. New York: Facts on
     File, 1986. 18-19.

For signed articles in reference books, begin with the author's name. For commonly known reference works (*Concise Columbia*), you need not include full publication information or editors' names. Page and volume numbers are also unnecessary when the entries in the reference book are arranged alphabetically.

19. Anonymous book

The End of a Presidency. New York: Bantam, 1974.

Alphabetically arrange anonymous books (and most other sources lacking an author name) in the Works Cited list by title, excluding *A*, *An*, or *The*.

20. Government document

United States. Cong. House. Committee on Energy and
    Commerce. Ensuring Access to Programming for the
    Backyard Satellite Dish Owner. Washington: GPO, 1986.

If the author is identified, begin with that name. If not, begin with the government (country or state), followed by the agency or organization. Most U.S. Government documents are printed/published by the Government Printing Office in Washington, DC. You may abbreviate this office *GPO*.

21. Dissertation

UNPUBLISHED

McGuire, Lisa C. "Adults' Recall and Retention of Medical
    Information." Diss. Bowling Green State University,
    1993.

Enclose the title of an unpublished dissertation in quotation marks, followed by the abbreviation "Diss." and the name of the university and the year.

PUBLISHED

Boothby, Daniel W. The Determinants of Earnings and
    Occupation for Young Women. Diss. U. of Cal., Berkeley,
    1978. New York: Garland, 1984.

For a published dissertation, underline the title, list the university and year as for an unpublished dissertation, and then add publication information as for a book, including the order number if the publisher is University Microfilms International (UMI). The descriptive abbreviation "diss." still follows the title.

22. A pamphlet

McKay, Hughina, and Mary Brown Patton. <u>Food Consumption of
    College Men</u>. Wooster: Ohio Agricultural Experiment
    Station, 1943.

Cite a pamphlet just as you cite a book. Remember the abbreviations *n.p.*, *n.d.*, and *n.pag.*, where publication information is missing. Also see item 23 below.

23. A book with missing publication information

Palka, Eugene, and Dawn M. Lake. <u>A Bibliography of Military
    Geography</u>. [New York?]: Kirby, [198-?].

The MLA practice is to provide missing publication information if possible. If the information you provide does not come from the source itself—that is, if you succeed in finding missing information through another source—you should enclose this information in brackets in the Works Cited entry [198–?]. If a date of publication can only be approximated, place a "c." before it, the abbreviation for the Latin *circa*, or "around." You may also use the abbreviations "n.p."—depending upon placement in your entry, this abbreviation stands for either "no place" or "no publisher"—"n.d." (no date), or "n. pag." (no pages).

24. TITLES WITHIN TITLE

Revard, Stella Purce. <u>The War in Heaven:</u> "Paradise Lost"
    <u>and the Tradition of Satan's Rebellion</u>. Ithaca, NY:
    Cornell UP, 1980.

McMahon, Robert. <u>The Two Poets of "Paradise Lost."</u> Baton
    Rouge: Louisiana State UP, 1998.

The MLA accepts two different ways of handling the titles of novels, plays, or other long works of fiction when such titles appear within the title of a book. The first entry above demonstrates the MLA's preferred method: Place quotation marks around but do not underline these titles within titles. The second entry above shows the other accepted style: The titles within titles are placed within quotation marks and are also underlined.

Documenting periodicals

25. Article, story, or poem in a monthly or bimonthly magazine

Hawn, Matthew. "Stay on the Web: Make Your Internet Site
    Pay Off." <u>Macworld</u> Apr. 1996: 94-98.

Abbreviate all months except May, June, and July. Hyphenate months for bimonthlies, and do not list volume or issue numbers.

26. Article, story, or poem in a weekly magazine

Updike, John. "His Mother Inside Him." <u>New Yorker</u> 20 Apr.
    1992: 34-36.

The publication date is inverted.

27. Article in a daily newspaper

Brody, Jane E. "Doctors Get Poor Marks for Nutrition
    Knowledge." <u>New York Times</u> 10 Feb. 1992, natl. ed.:
    B7.

Finn, Peter. "Death of a U-Va. Student Raises Scrutiny of
    Off-Campus Drinking." <u>Washington Post</u> 27 Sept. 1995:
    D1.

If an article in a newspaper is unsigned, begin with its title. Give the name of the newspaper as it appears on the masthead, excluding *A*, *An*, or *The*. If the city is not in the newspaper's name, it should follow the name in brackets: *Blade* [Toledo, OH]. Include with the page number the letter that designates any separately numbered sections; if sections are numbered consecutively, list the section number (sec. 2) before the colon, preceded by a comma.

28. Article in a journal paginated by volume

Nelson, Jennie. "This Was an Easy Assignment: Examining How
    Students Interpret Academic Writing Tasks." <u>Research in
    the Teaching of English</u> 34 (1990): 362-96.

If page numbers are continuous from one issue to the next throughout the year, include only the volume number and year, not the issue or month. For academic or professional journals, where volume numbers separate the journal title and the year of publication, MLA practice is to enclose the year in parentheses, reducing the potential for reader confusion.

29. Article in a journal paginated by issue

Tiffin, Helen. "Post-Colonialism, Post-Modernism, and the
    Rehabilitation of Post Colonial History." <u>Journal of
    Commonwealth Literature</u> 23.1 (1988): 169-81.

If each issue begins with page 1, include the volume number followed by a period and the issue number. Do not include the month of publication.

30. Anonymous article

"Fraternities Sue Hamilton College over Housing Rule." <u>The
    Chronicle of Higher Education</u>. 41.46 (1995): A39.

As with an anonymous book, if no author is listed for an article, begin your entry with the title and alphabetize by the first word, excluding *A*, *An*, and *The*.

31. Microform or microfiche article

Mayer, Caroline E. "Child-resistant Caps to Be Made 'Adult-friendly.' " <u>Washington Post</u> 16 June 1995: A3. CD-ROM. <u>NewsBank</u> (1995) CON 16: B17.

If the listing is derived from a computer-based reference source such as *News-bank*, which makes selected periodical articles available on microform or micro-fiche, you may treat it exactly as you would any other periodical. To help your audience locate the source as quickly as possible, however, unless it is just as easily located in printed form, you should include in your entry the descriptor *CD-ROM*, the name of the service (*NewsBank*), and the available section/grid information. See also the next section, "Documenting Electronic Sources."

32. Editorial

"Sarajevo Reborn." Editorial. <u>New York Times</u> 21 Feb. 1996, natl. ed.: A18.

" 'Blue' Makes Man Look Amazing." Editorial. <u>Dayton Daily News</u> 20 Feb. 1996: 6A.

If the editorial is signed, list the author's name first.

33. Letter to the editor and reply

Kempthorne, Charles. Letter. <u>Kansas City Star</u> 26 July 1992: A16.

Massing, Michael. Reply to letter of Peter Dale Scott. <u>New York Review of Books</u> 4 Mar. 1993: 57.

34. Review

Rev. of <u>Bone</u>, by Faye Myenne Ng. <u>New Yorker</u> 8 Feb. 1992: 113.

Rosen, Steven. "Dissing 'HIStory.' " Rev. of <u>HIStory: Past, Present, and Future-Book I,</u> by Michael Jackson. <u>Denver Post</u> 3 July 1995: F8.

Works Cited entries for reviews should begin with the reviewer's name, if known, followed by the title of the review, if there is one. Next the abbreviation "Rev. of" precedes the title of the work reviewed, which is followed by a comma, then the word "by" and the name of the work's author. If the work of an editor, translator, etc., is being reviewed instead an author's, an abbreviation such as "ed." or "trans." replaces the word "by." The entry concludes with standard publication information. If a review is unsigned and untitled, list it as "Rev. of _____" and alphabetize it by the name of the work reviewed. If the review is unsigned but titled, begin with the title. If the review is of a performance, add pertinent descriptive information such as director, composer, or major performers.

Documenting electronic sources

Research sources most often used by students from the World Wide Web include articles found in periodicals, texts of books, databases from reference sources, scholarly projects, and professional and personal sites.

The new edition of the *MLA Handbook* does not change the style for Internet citations, but it does expand the information to be included. The following citation exhibits the necessary components of an Internet citation.

①   ②
Hart, Francis R. "The Spaces of Privacy: Jane Austen."
· ·
Nineteenth-Century Fiction 30.3 (1975): 305–33.   ③
· ·
JSTOR. 5 Feb. 2003 <http://www.jstor.org/search>.
· ·
④   ⑤   ⑥

① Name of author, editor, translator, or compiler of the source.
② Title of the article or other short work, enclosed in quotation marks. For a posting to a discussion list or forum, use the subject line as the title.
③ Publication information for the print version of the source.
④ Title of the Internet site (scholarly project, database, online periodical, or Web site, underlined).
⑤ Date of access.
⑥ URL of the source or URL of the site's search page if the URL is exceptionally long

Remember to include the following details in your citation if such information is given or available for your source.

- Include the name of the editor, translator, or compiler of the source in addition to the author's name.
- Note the name of the editor of the Web site.
- Include the date of electronic publication, latest update, or posting.
- Give the name and location of the library if your site was accessed through a library subscription service.
- Name the list or forum, if your source is a posting to a discussion list or forum.
- Include the name of the site's sponsoring institution or organization.

Generally, you should consider the needs of your reader in documenting an electronic source, answering questions like these: Have I included enough data to give sufficient credit to the source? Is it clear what kind of source it is? Can my reader determine the validity of the source from the information I have provided? Can my reader easily access the source? If you are in doubt, your guideline should be to include more, not less, than is needed in the entry. Think of the entry as a place where all relevant and necessary information for understanding and locating a source is provided.

Two major kinds of online sources are important for researchers: one is the category that includes electronic newsletters, journals, and conferences; the other is electronic texts (literary works, scientific reports, historical documents, etc.).

Following MLA guidelines, Works Cited entries for electronic newsletters, journals, and conferences should be listed following the style of entries for articles in printed periodicals, with some additions: cite the author's name; the article or document title in quotation marks; the newsletter, journal, or conference title; the number of volume or issue; the year or date of publication (in parentheses); the number of pages or paragraphs (or "n. pag." if no pagination is given); the medium of publication ("Online"); the computer network name; and the date of access. The electronic address may be added to the end of the entry, preceded by "Available."

Entries for electronic texts should be listed following the style of a printed source, followed by the medium of publication ("Online"), the electronic text name (often a library or an archive), the computer network name, and the access date.

The 2003 MLA style sheet treats electronic publications in one of two ways, depending upon whether they are portable databases (those available in published form on CD-ROM diskettes or magnetic tape) or online databases (those accessible only through services or networks).

Portable databases are much like books and periodicals. Their entries in Works Cited lists are similar to those for printed material, except you must also include the following items:

- the medium of publication (CD-ROM, diskette, magnetic tape)
- the name of the vendor, if known (this may be different from the name of the organization that compiled the information, which must also be included)
- the date of electronic publication, in addition to the date the material originally may have been published (as for a reprinted book or article)

Online databases are not portable and are often updated, so their citations must also include the following items:

- medium of publication—specifically "Online"
- computer service or network name
- date of access, in addition to the date that the material originally may have been published (as for a reprinted book or article)

Following are general samples of documenting electronic sources. Note how each includes almost the same information and places the information in almost the same order.

35. Book

Austen, Jane. Emma. 1811. Litrix Reading Room. 2 Apr. 2003
    <http://www.litrix.com/emma/emma001.htm>.

36. Book in a scholarly project

Braddon, Mary Elizabeth. Lady Audley's Secret. 1862.
    Victorian Women Writers Project. Ed. Perry Willett.
    Indiana U. 3 April 2003 <http://www.indiana.edu/
    ~letrs.vwwp/braddon/lady1.html>.

37. Professional site

Project Zero. Home page. Harvard Graduate School of
    Education. 13 Nov. 2002 <http://pzweb.harvard.edu/
    Default.htm>.

38. Personal site

Roche, Jessica. Home page. June 2001. 13 Nov. 2002
    <http://www.lehigh.edu/~ineng/jbr2/
    jbr2-personalpage.htm>.

39. Government site

Home Education and Private Tutoring. Home page.
    Pennsylvania Department of Education. 17 Oct. 2002
    <http://www.pde.state.pa.us/home_education/site/
    default.asp>.

40. Academic home page

Art History. Dept. home page. Rutgers U. 2 Apr. 2003
    <http://arthistory.rutgers.edu/gradhome.htm>.

41. Course home page

Paul, Beth. Psychology of Gender. Course home page. Fall
    2002. Dept. of Psychology, The College of NJ.
    2 Apr. 2003 <http://paul.tcnj.edu/gender>.

42. Online work of art

Van Gogh, Vincent. <u>The Olive Trees</u>. 1889. Museum of Modern
    Art, New York. 5 Dec. 2001 <http://www.moma.org/docs/
    collection/paintsculpt/recent/c463.htm>.

43. Online film or film clip

Columbus, Chris, dir. <u>Harry Potter and the Sorcerer's
    Stone</u>. Trailer. Warner Brothers, 2001. 5 Dec. 2001
    <http://hollywood.com>.

44. Online cartoon

Bell, Darrin. "Rudy Park." Cartoon. <u>New York Times on the
    Web</u> 5 Dec. 2001. 5 Dec 2001 <http://www.uclick.com/
    client/nyt/rk>.

45. Electronic television or radio program

Chayes, Sarah. "Concorde." <u>All Things Considered</u>. Natl.
    Public Radio. 26 July 2000. 7 Dec. 2001
    <http://www.npr.com/programs/atc/archvies>.

46. Article in a online database

Haggerty, George E. "The Sacrifice of Privacy in Sense and
    Sensibility." <u>Tulsa Studies in Women's Literature</u> 7.2
    (1988): 221-37. <u>JSTOR</u>. 28 Mar. 2003 <http://
    ww.jstor.org/search>.

47. Article in a journal

Rowlinson, Hugh. "The Contribution of Count Rumford to
    Domestic Life in Jane Austen's Time." <u>Persuasions</u> 23.1
    (Winter 2002). 3 Apr. 2003 <http://www.jasna.org/
    po105/rowlinson.html>.

48. Article in a magazine

Purvis, Andrew. "In Search of a Lost Cruise Missile." <u>Time</u>
    1 April 2003. 2 Apr. 2003 <http://www.time.com/time/
    world/Article/0,8599,439517,00.html>.

49. Posting to a discussion list

Woodbury, Chuck. "Free RV Campgrounds." Online posting. 4
    Dec. 1999. The RV Home Page Bulletin Board. 13 Nov. 2002
    <http://www.rvhome.com/wwwboard/messages/4598.html>.

50. CD-ROM database, periodically updated

"U. S. Population by Age: Urban and Urbanized Areas." <u>1990</u>
    <u>U. S. Census of Population and Housing</u>. CD-ROM. US
    Bureau of the Census, 1990.

If a database comes from a printed source such as a book, periodical, or collection of bibliographies or abstracts, cite this information first, followed by the underlined title of the database, the medium of publication, the vendor name if applicable, and the date of electronic publication. If there is no printed source, include the title of the material accessed (in quotation marks), the date of the material if given, the underlined title of the database, the medium of publication, the vendor name if applicable, and the date of electronic publication. You may occasionally have difficulty determining some of the information requested in these guidelines; as for any other type of source, however, simply follow the guidelines as closely and consistently as possible.

51. CD-ROM, nonperiodical

<u>Myst</u>. CD-ROM. Novato, CA: Broderbund-Cyan, 1994.

"O'Keefe, Georgia." <u>The 1995 Grolier Encyclopedia</u>. CD-ROM.
    Danbury: Grolier, 1994.

List as you would a book, adding the medium of publication and information about the source, if applicable. If citing only part of a work, underline the title of this portion or place it within quotation marks, as appropriate (as you would a printed short story, poem, article, essay, or similar source).

52. Diskettes

Greco, Diane. <u>Cyborg: Engineering the Body Electric</u>.
    Diskette. Watertown: Eastgate, 1996.

Lanham, Richard D. <u>The Electronic Word: Democracy,
    Technology, and the Arts</u>. Diskette. Chicago: U of
    Chicago P, 1993.

List in the Works Cited as you would a book, adding the medium of publication (e.g., "Diskette") and information about the printed source, if available.

53. Electronic texts

Melville, Herman. <u>Moby Dick</u>. New York: Hendricks House,
    1952. Online. U of Virginia Lib. Internet. 6 Jan.
    1996.

"Visible Human Project Fact Sheet." <u>Visibile Human Project</u>.
    Bethesda: National Library of Medicine, 1995: n. pag.
    National Library of Medicine. 10 Feb. 1996 <Gopher:
    gopher.nlm.gov:70/00/visible/visibletxt>.

Entries for electronic texts should include, as possible, the author's name, the title of the work, original (printed) publication information, publication medium ("Online"), repository of the online text (name of the online library), name of the computer network, and the date you "accessed" or read the text. If you access an electronic text by its URL(as you may with Gopher databases and electronic texts on the web), give the access date followed by the URLenclosed in angle brackets.

54. E-mail messages

Fallon, John. "Re: EECAP Summer Seminar." E-mail to John
    Clark. 6 Feb. 2003.

Krause, Steven. "Rejoining the Conversation." E-mail to the
    Rhetnet listserv. 25 Jan. 2002.

E-mail messages are presented in the Works Cited very much as a personal letter would be listed. Included the name of the sender (in the author position); the title (subject line), where available, enclosed in quotation marks; a message description which includes the recipient; and the date of the message.

55. Public postings on electronic networks

Davis, Gracie. "Facts about Tori and Eric." Online Posting.
    20 Feb. 1996: n. pag. 27 Feb. 1996
    <news:rec.music.tori-amos.Usetnet>.

Haneef, Omar. "Question on Nietzsche." Online posting. 21
    Feb. 1996: n. pag. 27 Feb. 1996 <news:
    aH.postmoder.Usenet>.

To list public online postings, include the author's name, the title of the posting, the date of posting, the description "Online posting," the name of the newsgroup or forum where you found the posting, the name of the network, and the date of access. Common forums for public online postings include bulletin boards, commercial online services, and Usenet groups, all of which are asynchronous, or non-real-time discussion formats.

56. Synchronous communication

Bleck, Bradley. Online discussion of "Virtual First Year
    Composition: Distance Education, the Internet, and the
    World Wide Web." 8 June 1997. DaMOO. 27 Feb. 1999.
    <http://DaMOO.csun.edu/CW/brad.html>.

Generally follow the guidelines for other online citations, modifying them wherever necessary, but always provide as much information as possible. Some cited material will require identifying labels (e.g., *Interview* or *Online posting*), but such labels should be neither underlined nor set within quotation marks. When documenting synchronous communications that are posted in MOO (multi-user domain, object oriented) and MUD (multi-user domain) forums, name the speaker or speakers; describe the event; provide the date of the event and the name of the forum (e.g. linguaMOO); and cite the date of access as well as the network name (including the prefix TELNET://).

57. Work from a library or personal subscription service

Dwyer, Jim. "Cheers and smiles for U.S. Troops in a
    Captured City." New York Times 2 Apr. 2003 New York
    Times Online. America Online. 3 Apr. 2003. Keyword:
    nytimes.

Stewart, Doug, Lisa Drew, and Mark Wexler. "Diary of a
    Century: How Conservation Grew From a Whisper to a
    Roar." National Wildlife 38.1 (Dec. 1999-Jan. 2000): 1-
    22. ProQuest Direct. Teaneck Public Library, Teaneck,
    NJ. 7 Dec. 1999 <http://proquest.umi.com>.

For works that have been assessed through an online service, either through a library service (e.g., ProQuest Direct or Lexis-Nexis) or through one of the large Internet providers (e.g., America Online), you may not know the URL of the source. In such cases, cite the keyword or path that led to the source, if applicable, and separate each individual item in the path with a semicolon; the keyword or path will be the last item in the citation. For sources assessed through library services, as above, cite the name of the service, the name and location of the library, the date you assessed the material, and the URL of the service's home page. If you also know the name of the database used, include that information (underlined) before the name of the online service.

58. Software programs

WordPerfect for Macintosh. Vers. 3.5 CD-ROM. Orem, UT:
    Novell, 1995.

List as you would a book, adding other information (e.g., version number, medium of publication, information about the printed source) as applicable.

59. Publication on magnetic tape

English Poetry Full-Text Database. Rel. 2. Magnetic tape.
   Cambridge, Eng.: Chadwyck, 1993.

List as you would a book; the conventions are comparable to those for software programs.

60. Publication in more than one medium

Perseus 1.0: Interactive Sources and Studies on Ancient
   Greece. CD-ROM videodisc. New Haven: Yale UP, 1992.

List in Works Cited as you would a nonperiodical CD-ROM publication, adding information on all media making up the work.

61. Other online materials with URLs

FTP

Hart, Michael. "Short FAQ." Project Gutenberg. (1995): n.
   pag. 24 Feb. 1996. <FTP: mrcnext.cso.uiuc.edu/pub/
   etext/gutenberg/articles>.

Williams, Mathew. Autoflow. (1994). n. pag. Hypercard
   stack. 2 Feb. 1996. <FTP: dartmouth.edu/pub/
   hypertexts>.

GOPHER

Clinton, William. "Remarks by the President at the Tribute
   Dinner for Senator Byrd." Washington: Office of the
   White House Press Secretary, 17 July 1994: n. pag. 27
   Feb. 1996. <Gopher: info.amu.edu.70/00/.data/
   politics/1994/byrd.0717>.

Darwin, Charles. The Voyage of the BeagleM. Harvard
   Classics Vol. 29. New York: Collier, 1909. Rel. Sep.
   1993. Wiretap Electronic Library. 2 Mar. 1996 <Gopher:
   wiretap.spies.com.70/00/Library/Classic/beagle.txt>.

ONLINE CHAT SESSIONS (E.G., IRC/MUD/MOO)

Callis, Rhonda. "Virtual Class Meeting." CollegeTown MOO.
   Online. Internet. 14 Apr. 1994 <Telnet: patty.bvu.edu>.

StoneHenger. Personal Interview. <u>The Glass Dragon MOO</u>. 6
    Feb. 1995 <Telnet: surf.tstc.edu>.

TELNET

King, Jr., Martin Luther. "I Have a Dream Speech." N.p.:
    n.p., (28 Aug. 1963): n. pag. 3 Jan. 1996 <Telnet:
    ukanaix.cc.ukans.edu>.

"1993 University Guide to NASA." N.p.: National Aeronautics
    and Space Administration, 15 Feb. 1993: n. pag. 20
    Feb. 1996. <Telnet: spacelink.msfc.nasa.gov>.

Documenting other sources

62. Cartoon

Davis, Jim. "Garfield." Cartoon. <u>Courier</u> [Findlay, OH] 17
    Feb. 1996; E4.

Roberts, Victoria. Cartoon. <u>New Yorker</u> 13 July 1992: 34.

63. Film, videocassette or DVD

<u>Casablanca</u>. Dir. Michael Curtiz. Perf. Humphrey Bogart and
    Ingrid Bergman. Warner Bros., 1942.

<u>Fast Food: What's in It for You?</u> Prod. The Center for
    Science in the Public Interest and Churchill Films.
    Videocassette. Los Angeles: Churchill, 1988.

Begin with the title, followed by the director, the studio, and the year released.
Optionally, you may include the names of lead actors, producer, and the like
between the title and the distribution information. If your essay is concerned with
a particular person's work on a film, lead with that person's name, arranging all
other information accordingly.

Lewis, Joseph H., dir. <u>Gun Crazy</u>. Screenplay by Dalton
    Trumbo. King Bros., 1950.

64. Personal interview

Holden, James. Personal interview. 12 Jan. 2003.

Morser, John. Professor of Political Science, U of
    Wisconsin. Telephone interview. 15 Dec. 2001.

Begin with the interviewee's name and specify the kind of interview and the date. Identify the interviewee's position if relevant to the purpose of the interview.

65. Published or broadcast interview

Sowell, Thomas. "Affirmative Action Programs." Interview.
    All Things Considered. NPR. WGTE, Toledo. 5 June 1990.

Steinglass, David. Interview. Counterpoint 7 May 1970: 3-4.

For published or broadcast interviews, begin with the interviewee's name. Include appropriate publication information for a periodical or book and appropriate broadcast information for a radio or television program.

66. Print advertisement

Cadillac DeVille. Advertisement. New York Times 21 Feb.
    1996, natl. ed.: A20.

Begin with the name of the product, followed by the description "Advertisement" and normal publication information for the source.

67. Unpublished lecture, public address, or speech

Graves, Donald. "When Bad Things Happen to Good Ideas."
    National Council of Teachers of English Convention. St.
    Louis, 21 Nov. 1989.

Begin with the speaker, followed by the title (if any), the meeting (and sponsoring organization, if needed), the location, and the date. If it is untitled, use a descriptive label (such as "Speech") with no quotation marks.

68. Personal or unpublished letter

Friedman, Paul. Letter to the author. 18 Mar. 1992.

Personal letters and e-mail messages are handled nearly identically in Works Cited entries. Begin with the name of the writer, identify the type of communication (e.g., "Letter"), and specify the audience. Include the date written if known, and the date received if not. To cite an unpublished letter from an archive or private collection, include information that locates the holding (for example, "Quinn-Adams Papers. Lexington Historical Society. Lexington, KY.").

69. Published letter

King, Jr., Martin Luther. "Letter from Birmingham City
    Jail." 28 Aug. 1963. Civil Disobedience in Focus. Ed.
    Hugo Adam Bedau. New York: Routledge, 1991. 68-84.

Cite published letters as you would a selection from an anthology. Specify the audience in the letter title (if known). Include the date of the letter immediately after its title. Place the page number(s) after the publisher information. If you cite more than one letter from a collection, cite the entire work in Works Cited and indicate individual dates and page numbers in your text.

70. Map

<u>Ohio River: Foster, KY to New Martinsville, WV</u>. Map.
    Huntington: U. S. Corps of Engineers, 1985.

Cite a map as you would a book by an unknown author. Underline the title and identify it as a map or chart.

71. Performance

Bissex, Rachel. Folk Songs. Flynn Theater. Burlington, VT.
    14 May 1990.

<u>Rumors</u>. By Neil Simon. Dir. Gene Saks. Broadhurst Theater,
    New York. 17 Nov. 1988.

Identify the pertinent details such as title, place, and date of performance. If you focus on a particular person in your essay, such as the director or conductor, lead with that person's name. For a recital or individual concert, lead with the performer's name.

72. Audio recording

Young, Neil, comp. perf. <u>Mirror Ball</u>. CD. In part
    accompanied by members of Pearl Jam. Burbank, CA:
    Reprise, 1995.

Marley, Bob, and the Wailers. "Buffalo Soldier." <u>Legend</u>.
    Audiocassette. Island Records, 1984.

Depending upon the focus of your essay, begin with the artist, composer, or conductor. Enclose song titles in quotation marks, followed by the recording title, underlined. Do not underline musical compositions identified only by form, number, and key. If you are not citing a compact disc, specify the recording format. End with the company label, the catalog number (if known), and the date of issue.

73. Television or radio broadcast

"Emissary." <u>Star Trek: Deep Space Nine</u>. Teleplay by Michael
    Pillar. Story by Rick Berman and Michael Pillar. Dir.
    David Carson. Fox. WFLX, West Palm Beach, FL. 9 Jan.
    1993.

If the broadcast is not an episode of a series or the episode is untitled, begin with the program title. Include the network, the station and city, and the date of broadcast. The inclusion of other information-such as narrator, writer, director, or performers—depends on the purpose of your citation.

74. Work of art

Holbein, Hans. <u>Portrait of Erasmus</u>. The Louvre, Paris. The
    Louvre Museum. By Germain Bazin. New York: Abrams,
    n.d., 148.

McIntyre, Linda. <u>Colors</u>. Art Institute of Chicago.

Begin with the artist's name. Follow with the title, and conclude with the location. If your source is a book, also give pertinent publication information.

TITLE
CENTERED,
ONE-THIRD
DOWN
PAGE

The Two Freedoms of Henry David Thoreau

by

NAME   Andrew Turner

INSTUCTOR   Professor Stephany

COURSE   English 2

DATE   3 October 2002

↑
1"
↓

1"

1/2"

DOUBLE SPACED

WRITER'S LAST NAME AND PAGE NUMBER APPEAR ON EACH PAGE.

The Two Freedoms of Henry David Thoreau

Henry David Thoreau led millions of people throughout the world to think about individual freedom in a new way. During his lifetime, he attempted to live free of unjust governmental constraints as well as contentional social expectations. In his 1849 essay "On the Duty of Civil Disobedience," he makes his strongest case against governmental interference in the lives of citizens. In his 1854 book Walden, or, Life in the Woods, he makes the case for living free from social conventions and expectations.

WRITER OPENS WITH THESIS.

WRITER IDENTIFIES TWO WORKS TO BE EXAMINED.

ONLY THE PAGE NUMBER IS NEEDED WHEN SOURCE IS INTRODUCED IN THE SENTENCE.

Thoreau opens "Civil Disobedience" with his statement that "that government is best which governs not at all" (222). He argues that a government should allow its people to be as free as possible, providing for the needs of the people without infringing on their daily lives. Thoreau explains, "The government does not concern me much, and I shall bestow the fewest possible thoughts on it. It is not for many moments that I live under a government" ("Civil" 238). In other words, in his daily life he attends to his business of eating, sleeping, and earning a living and not dealing in any noticeable way with an entity called "a government."

ABBREVIATED TITLE IS USED AFTER WORK HAS BEEN IDENTIFIED BY FULL TITLE.

SHORT TITLE IS ADDED TO PAGE NUMBER BECAUSE TWO WORKS BY SAME AUTHOR APPEAR ON WORKS CITED PAGE.

Because Thoreau did not want his freedom overshadowed by governmental regulations, he tried

to ignore them. However, the American government of 1845 would not let him. He was arrested
and put in the Concord jail for failing to pay
his poll tax-a tax he believed unjust because
it supported the government's war with Mexico
as well as the immoral institution of slavery.
Instead of protesting his arrest, he celebrated
it and explained its meaning by writing "Civil
Disobedience," one of the most famous English-
language essays ever written. In it, he argued
persuasively that "Under a government which
imprisons any unjustly, the true place for a
just man is also a prison" (230). Thus the doctrine of passive resistance was formed, a doctrine that advocated protest against the
government by nonviolent means:

> How does it become a man to behave
> toward this American government
> today? I answer that he cannot
> without disgrace be associated with
> it. I cannot for an instant recog-
> nize that political organization as
> my government which is the slave's
> government also. (224)

According to Charles R. Anderson,
Thoreau's other writings, such as "Slavery in
Massachusetts" and "A Plea for Captain John
Brown," show his disdain of the "northerners
for their cowardice on conniving with such an
institution" (28). He wanted all free American
citizens, north and south, to revolt and liber-
ate the slaves.

Works Cited

WORK WITH MORE THAN THREE AUTHORS IS CITED WITH FIRST AUTHOR'S NAME AND "ET AL."

Anderson, Charles Roberts, ed. <u>Thoreau's</u>
<u>Vision: The Major Essays.</u> Englewood
Cliffs, NJ: Prentice Hall, 1973.

DOUBLE-SPACED

Spiller, Robert E., et al. <u>Literary</u>
<u>History of the United States:</u>
<u>History</u>. 3rd ed. New York: Macmil-
lan, 1963.

Thoreau, Henry David. "On the Duty of
Civil Disobedience." <u>Walden and</u>
<u>Civil Disobedience</u>. New York: NAL,
1960.

←1"→

FORMAT FOR WORKS WITHIN AN ANTHOLOGY

—-. <u>Walden, or, Life in the Woods. Walden</u>
<u>and Civil Disobedience</u>. New York: ←1"→
NAL, 1960.

INDENTED 5 SPACES

3

Documenting Sources:
Chicago Manual Style (CMS)

The most widely used documentation style in history, philosophy, religion, and fine arts is the bibliographic note style found in *The Chicago Manual of Style*, 14th edition, published by the University of Chicago Press (Chicago: 1993). Although bibliographic notes may be somewhat more cumbersome for writers and scholars than in-text citation systems, they hinder or distract readers less. Sample pages using the CMS biblographic notes are provided at the end of this chapter.

1 Conventions for Marking In-Text Citations

Each time you quote, paraphrase, or summarize source material in your text, you need to mark it by inserting a raised (superscript) Arabic number immediately after the sentence or clause containing the information. The superscript number must follow all punctuation except dashes. Each new reference to source material requires a new number, and numbers are arranged consecutively throughout the text.

```
Frank Lloyd Wright's "prairie style" was characterized
initially by the houses he built around Chicago "with low
horizontal lines echoing the landscape."[1] Vincent Scully
sees the suburban building lots for which Wright was
designing as one of the architect's most important
influences.[2]
```

Each superscript number corresponds to a note at the end of the paper, or sometimes at the foot of the page on which the number appears.

```
1. The Concise Columbia Encyclopedia, S.V. "Wright, Frank
Lloyd.".

2. Vincent Scully, Architecture: The Natural and the
Manmade (New York: St. Martin's, 1991), 340.
```

2 Conventions for Positioning Notes and Bibliographies

Endnotes are typed as a single list at the end of a text. Endnotes are easier to format than footnotes since they can be typed separately on a sheet of paper without calculating the space needed on each page. Some word processing programs have a built-in footnote-formatting function, but endnotes are more convenient and efficient for the person who is preparing the final paper.

Directory for CMS Bibliographic Notes

DOCUMENTING BOOKS: FIRST REFERENCE

1. Book by one author
2. Book by two or more authors
3. Revised edition of a book
4. Edited book and one volume of a multivolume book
5. Translated book
6. Reprinted book
7. Work in an anthology or chapter in an edited collection
8. Article in a reference book
9. Anonymous book

DOCUMENTING PERIODICALS: FIRST REFERENCE

10. Article, story, or poem in a monthly or bimonthly magazine
11. Article, story, or poem in a weekly magazine
12. Article in a daily newspaper
13. Article in a journal paginated by volume
14. Article in ajournal paginated by issue
15. Review

DOCUMENTING ELECTRONIC SOURCES: FIRST REFERENCE

16. Material on CD-ROM database, periodically updated
17. Material on diskette
18. E-mail and other electronic messages
19. Materials accessed via networks

DOCUMENTING OTHER SOURCES: FIRST REFERENCE

20. Personal interview
21. Personal or unpublished letter
22. Work of art

DCOUMENTING SUBSEQUENT REFERENCES TO THE SAME WORK

23. Subsequent references to a work

The **endnote page** follows the last page of text and is numbered in sequence with the rest of the paper. Title the first page of the endnote section "Notes"—centered, without quotation marks, and one inch from the top of the page. Double-space throughout—between this title and the first entry, within the notes or entries themselves, and between entries. Order your entries consecutively according to the note numbers in your paper. Indent the first line of each entry five spaces from the left margin, and place each subsequent entry line flush with the margin.

Footnotes are more convenient for readers, because instead of turning to the back of a text to check a numbered source, they can find the information simply by glancing at the bottom of the page they are reading. Footnotes must always be placed at the bottom of the same page on which the marker-number appears, four lines below the last line of text and single-spaced.

Some instructors and/or programs require a separate, alphabetically arranged list of sources, or **bibliography**, in addition to endnotes or footnotes. If so, follow the MLA guidelines for a list of Works Cited. (See page 22.) If you are asked to include in your bibliography only sources consulted in researching for your paper, title your bibliography list "Works Consulted."

3 Conventions for Endnote and Footnote Format

Different style manuals offer a number of minor variations for the format of endnotes and footnotes. The following guidelines are based on *The Chicago Manual of Style*.

Numbers and spacing. Each entry is preceded by an Arabic number with a period that is indented five spaces and followed by a space. Any subsequent lines for an entry begin at the left margin. Double-space endnotes throughout. Single-space individual footnotes and double-space between footnotes.

Authors. List all authors' names first name first, spelling them as they appear in their book. You may spell out the first name or use initials.

Punctuation. Separate authors' names and all titles with commas, and enclose all book publication information and periodical dates in parentheses. Use colons to separate the place of publication from the publisher and commas to separate the publisher from the date. Colons should also be used to separate journal dates from page numbers. End all entries with a period.

Page numbers. Each entry for a book or periodical should end with the page number(s) on which the cited information can be found. (Note that in CMS, "p." or "pp." is used with the actual page number for material from journals that do not use volume numbers.)

The following are examples of the most common endnote citations required in undergraduate humanities papers.

Documenting Books: First Reference

1. Book by one author

1. Jessica Benjamin, <u>The Bonds of Love: Psychoanalysis,</u>
<u>Feminism, and the Problem of Domination</u> (New York:
Prometheus, 1988), 76.

2. Book by two or more authors

2. Richard L. Zweigenhaft and G. William Domhoff, <u>Blacks</u>
<u>in the White Establishment</u> (New Haven: Yale University
Press, 1991), 113.

For three or more authors, follow each name with a comma.

3. Revised edition of a book

3. S. I. Hayakawa, <u>Language in Thought and Action</u>, 4th
ed. (New York: Harcourt, 1978), 77.

4. Edited book and one volume of a multivolume book

4. Tom Waldrep, ed., <u>Writers on Writing</u>, vol. 2 (New
York: Random House, 1988), 123.

5. Translated book

5. Albert Camus, <u>The Stranger</u>, trans. Stuart Gilbert (New
York: Random House, 1946), 12.

6. Reprinted book

6. Elizabeth E. G. Evans, <u>The Abuse of Maternity</u> (1875;
reprint, New York: Arno, 1974), 74-78.

7. Work in an anthology or chapter in an edited collection

7. Mona Charen, "Much More Nasty Than They Should Be," in
<u>Popular Writing in America: The Interaction of Style and</u>
<u>Audience</u>, 5th ed., ed. Donald McQuade and Robert Atwan (New
York: Oxford University Press, 1993), 207-8.

8. Article in a reference book

8. "Langella, Frank," <u>International Television and Video Almanac</u>, 40th ed. (New York: Quigley, 1995).

No page number is needed for an alphabetically arranged book. Begin the entry with the author's name, if available. For well known reference books, such as the *Merriam-Webster Dictionary*, follow example number 1, page 52.

9. Anonymous book

9. <u>The World Almanac and Book of Facts</u> (New York: World Almanac-Funk & Wagnalls, 1995).

Documenting Periodicals: First Reference

10. Article, story, or poem in a monthly or bimonthly magazine

10. Matthew Hawn, "Stay on the Web: Make Your Internet Site Pay Off," <u>Macworld</u>, April 1996, 94-98.

11. Article, story, or poem in a weekly magazine

11. John Updike, "His Mother Inside Him," <u>New Yorker</u>, 20 April 1992, 34.

12. Article in a daily newspaper

12. Peter Finn, "Death of a U-Va. Student Raises Scrutiny of Off-Campus Drinking," <u>Washington Post</u>, 27 September 1995, sec. D, p. 1.

13. Article in a journal paginated by volume

13. Jennie Nelson, "This Was an Easy Assignment: Examining How Students Interpret Academic Writing Tasks," <u>Research in the Teaching of English</u> 34 (1990): 362-96.

14. Article in a journal paginated by issue

14. Helen Tiffin, "Post-Colonialism, Post-Modernism, and the Rehabilitation of Post Colonial History," <u>Journal of Commonwealth Literature</u> 23, no. 1 (1988): 169-81.

15. Review

15. Review of <u>Bone</u>, by Faye Myenne Ng, <u>New Yorker</u>, 8 February 1992, 113.

16. Steven Rosen, "Dissing 'HIStory,' " review of <u>HIStory: Past, Present, and Future-Book I</u>, by Michael Jackson, <u>Denver Post</u>, 3 July 1995, sec. F, p. 8.

Documenting Electronic Sources: First Reference

The editors of the University of Chicago plan to provide extensive coverage of documenting electronic sources in the 15th edition of the *Manual*, due sometime early in the 21st century. The current (14th) edition subscribes to the International Standards Organization (ISO), which stresses consistency while offering greater flexibility in such matters as typeface, punctuation, capitalizing, and underlining. ISO citation system information may be requested from

ISO TC46/SC9
Secretariat: Office of Library Standards
National Library of Canada
Ottawa K1A 0N4 Canada

16. Material on CD-ROM database, periodically updated

17. <u>Oregon Trail II, Ver. 1.0 Mac</u> [CD-ROM]. Minneapolis: Educational Computing Corp., 1995. ERIC, SilverPlatter, March 1996.

17. Material on diskette

18. Diane Greco, Cyborg: Engineering the Body Electric <u>[Disk]. Watertown: Eastgate, 1996.</u>

18. E-mail and other electronic messages

19. John Fallon, "Re: EECAP Sumemr Seminar," e-mail to John Clark, 6 February 1996.

19. Materials accessed via networks

20. Jerry Gray, "In Congress, G.O.P. Ponders Tactics to Regain the Edge," <u>The New York Times on the Web</u> [online] (25 February 1996), INTERNET.

21. Herman Melville, Moby Dick [online] (New York: Hendricks House, 1952), University of Virginia Library, 6 January 1996, INTERNET.

22. "Visible Human Project Fact Sheet," Visible Human Project [online] (Bethesda: National Library of Medicine, 1995), National Library of medicine, 10 February 1996, INTERNET.

Documenting Other Sources: First Reference

20. Personal interview

23. John Morser, interview by author, Chicago, 15 December 1993.

21. Personal or unpublished letter

24. Paul Friedman, letter to author, 18 March 1992.

If the letter is in a collection, provide the pertinent information about where it may be found, after the date.

22. Work of art

25. Hans Holbein, Portrait of Erasmus, The Louvre, Paris, in The Louvre Museum, by Germain Bazin (New York: Abrams, n.d.), p. 148.

Documenting Subsequent References to the Same Work

23. Subsequent references to a work

In CMS, after you have referred to a source once, in subsequent notes include the author's last name, a comma, a shortened version of the title, another comma, and the page number(s). On page 52, notes 1 and 6 give the form for the first references to the Benjamin and Evans works.

26. Benjamin, Bonds, 76.

27. Evans, The Abuse, 74–78.

The traditional Latin abbreviations *ibid.* ("in the same place") and *op cit.* ("in the work cited") are seldom used in contemporary scholarly writing.

4 Conventions For a Separate Bibliography

When you use CMS notes to document sources, a separate list of references is not needed, but it may be a convenience for your readers or a requirement for your course. Include the following information.

For a book,

1. The name(s) of the author, editors, or organization which wrote the book
2. The complete book title and subtitle, if it has one
3. If the book is part of a series, the title of the series and volume(s) numbers
4. If the book is published in multiple volumes, the volume number or total number of volumes
5. The edition, if the book is not the first edition
6. The city where the book was published
7. The name of the publisher (this is sometimes omitted)
8. The date when the book was published

For an article in a periodical,

1. The author(s) name
2. The article title
3. The periodical's name
4. The volume number of the periodical (and, in some instances, the issue number)
5. The date the periodical was issued
6. The page numbers in the periodical where the article occurs

Be aware that the *Chicago Manual* also has a "parenthetical" name-date documentation style that is used in disciplines other than those in the humanities. It requires a list of references, which are formatted somewhat differently than the list of references that may be used with bibligraphic notes.

Book

Author's Last Name, First Name. <u>Title of the Book:
    Subtitle</u>. City: Publisher, date.

Durant, Will. <u>The Story of Civilization: Our Oriental
    Heritage</u>. New York: MJF Books, 1935.

Journal

Author's Last Name, First Name. "Title of the Article."
    <u>Title of the Periodical</u> volume number (date): page
    numbers.

Norko, Juliet M. "Hawthorne's Love Letters: The Threshold

World of Sophia Peabody." <u>American Transcendental Quarterly</u>
    7 (1993): 127-39.

For the natural and social sciences, the basic style looks like this:

Book

Author's Last Name, Initials. Date. <u>Title of the book:</u>
    <u>Subtitle</u>. City: Publisher.

Jones, R. M. 1994. <u>The Behavior of Bats</u>. Cambridge: Harvard
    University Press.

Journal

Author's Last Name, Initials. Date. Title of the article.
    <u>Title of the Periodical</u> volume number:page number(s).

Perssons, L. 1997. New Hubble Discoveries. <u>Nature</u>
    278:315-31.

Sample page with endnotes

recorded "in exultant tones the universal neglect that
had overtaken pagan learning."[2] It would be some time,
however, before Christian education would replace
classical training, and by the fourth century, a lack
of interest in learning and culture among the elite of
Roman society was apparent. Attempting to check the
demise of education, the later emperors established
municipal schools, and universities of rhetoric and
law were also established in major cites throughout
the Empire.[3]

Notes

1. Rosamond McKitterick, The Carolingians and the
Written Word (Cambridge: Cambridge University
Press,1983), 61.

2. J. Bass Mullinger, The Schools of Charles the
Great (New York: Stechert, 1911), 10.

3. James W. Thompson, The Literacy of the Laity in
the Middle Ages (New York: Franklin, 1963), 17.

4. O. M. Dalton, introduction, The Letters of Sidonius
(Oxford: Clarendon, 1915), cxiv.

5. Pierre Riche, Education and Culture in the
Barbarian West (Columbia: University of South
Carolina Press, 1976), 4.

6. Riche, Education and Culture, 6.

The Teatro Olímpico was completed in 1584, the statues, inscriptions, and bas-reliefs for the frons-scena being the last details completed. Meanwhile, careful plans were made for an inaugural which was to be a production of Oedipus in a new translation.[10] Final decisions were made by the Academy in February of 1585 for the seating of city officials, their wives, and others, with the ruling that "no masked men or women would be allowed in the theatre for the performance."[11]

The organization of the audience space was "unique among Renaissance theaters, suggesting . . . its function as the theater of a 'club of equals' rather than of a princely court."[12] The Academy is celebrated and related to Roman grandeur by the decorating over the monumental central opening, where its motto, "Hoc Opus," appears.[13] It is difficult to make out the entrances

10. J. Thomas Oosting, Andrea Palladio's Teatro Olímpico (Ann Arbor, MI: UMI Research Press, 1981), 118-19.

11. Oosting, Palladio's Teatro, 120.

12. Marvin Carlson, Places of Performance: The Semiotics of Theater Architecture (Ithaca, N.Y.: Cornell University Press, 1989), 135.

13. Simon Tidworth, Theaters: An Architectural and Cultural History (London: Praeger, 1973), 52.

Sample Bibliography

Bibliography

Dalton, O.M. Introduction to <u>The Letters of Sidonius</u>.
     Oxford: Clarendon, 1915.

McKittrick, Rosamond. <u>The Carolingians and the Written
     Word</u>. Cambridge: Cambridge University Press, 1983.

Mullinger, J. Bass. <u>The Schools of Charles the Great</u>.
     New York: Stechert, 1911.

Riche, Pierre. <u>Education and Culture in the Barbarian
     West</u>. Columbia: University of South Carolina
     Press, 1976.

Thompson, James W. <u>The Literacy of the Laity in the
     Middle Ages</u>. New York: Franklin, 1963.

4
Documenting Sources: APA Guidelines

Most disciplines in the social sciences—psychology, sociology, anthropology, political science, and economics—use the name-and-date system of documentation put forth by the American Psychological Association (APA). The disciplines of education and business also use this system. This citation style highlights dates of publication because the currency of published material is of primary importance in these disciplines. Also, listing author names has been more strongly emphasized in the APA than in the MLA system; collaborative authoring is common in the social sciences, and it is the APA convention to recognize the efforts of the first six collaborators. For more about the foundations and purposes the APA system, see the *Publication Manual of the American Psychological Association*, 5th ed. (Washington, DC: APA, 2001). The numbered entries that follow introduce and explain some of the conventions of this system.

Directory for APA Documentation Guidelines

CONVENTIONS FOR IN-TEXT CITATIONS

1. Single work by one or more authors
2. Two or more works by the same author published in the same year
3. Unknown author
4. Corporate or organizational author
5. Authors with the same last name
6. Quote from an indirect source
7. More than one work in a citation
8. Long quote set off from text
9. Electronic source

CONVENTIONS FOR FOOTNOTES

CONVENTIONS FOR THE REFERENCES PAGE

DOCUMENTING BOOKS

1. Book by one author
2. Book by two or more authors
3. More than one book by the same author
4. Book by a corporation, association, or organization
5. Revised edition of a book

---

1 Conventions for In-Text Citations

1. Single work by one or more authors

Whenever you quote, paraphrase, or summarize material in your text, you should give both the author's last name and the date of the source. For direct quotations, you must also provide specific page numbers, if applicable. You may also provide page references, as a convenience to your readers, whenever you suspect they might want to consult a source you have cited. Page references in the APA system are always preceded, in-text or in the References, by the abbreviation "p." for a single page or "pp." For multiple pages.

APA style requires that, authors' names, publication dates, and page numbers (when listed) should be placed in parentheses following citable material. If any of these elements are identified in the text referred to in the parenthetical citation, they are not repeated in the citation.

```
Exotoxins make some bacteria dangerous to humans
(Thomas, 1974).

According to Thomas (1974), "Some bacteria are only
harmful to us if they make exotoxins" (p. 76).

We need fear some bacteria only "if they make
exotoxins" (Thomas, 1974, p. 76).
```

For a work by **two authors**, cite both names.

```
Smith and Hawkins (1990) agree that all bacteria
producing exotoxins are harmful to humans.

All known exotoxin-producing bacteria are harmful to
humans (Smith & Hawkins, 1990).
```

The authors' names are joined by *and* within your text, but APA convention requires an ampersand (&) to join authors' names in parentheses.

For a work by **three to five authors**, identify all the authors by last name the first time you cite a source. In subsequent citations identify only the first author followed by "et al." ("and others").

```
The most recent study supports the belief that alcohol
abuse is on the rise (Dinkins, Dominic, Smith, Rogers,
& White, 1989). . . . When homeless people were excluded
from the study, the results were the same (Dinkins et
al., 1989).
```

If you are citing a source by **six or more authors**, identify only the first author in all in-text citations, followed by "et al." (The first six authors are named in the References list, however; see model 2 under "Documenting Books" for more details.)

2. Two or more works by the same author published in the same year

To distinguish between two or more works published in the same year by the same author or team of authors, place a lowercase letter (a, b, c, etc.), immediately after the date. This letter should correspond to that in the References list, where the entries will be alphabetized by title. If two appear in one citation, repeat the year.

```
(Smith, 1992a, 1992b)
```

3. Unknown author

To cite the work of an unknown author, use the first two or three words of the entry as it is listed on the References page (usually by the title). If the words are from the title, enclose them in quotation marks for the title of a periodical article, or italicize them for the title of a nonperiodical, whichever is appropriate.

```
Many researchers now believe that treatment should not
begin until other factors have been dealt with ("New
Evidence Suggests," 1987).
```

```
Statistical Abstracts (1991) reports the literacy rate
for Mexico at 75% for 1990, up 4% from census figures
10 years ago.
```

4. Corporate or organizational author

When a citation refers to a work by a corporation, association, organization, or foundation, spell out the name of the authoring agency. If the name can be abbreviated and remain identifiable, spell out the name only the first time it is cited, placing its abbreviation immediately after it, in brackets. For subsequent references to that source, you may use only the abbreviation.

```
(American Psychological Association [APA], 1993)
```

```
(APA, 1994)
```

5. Authors with the same last name

To avoid confusion when citing two or more authors with the same last name, always include each author's initials in every citation.

```
(C. L. Clark, 1994; J. M. Clark, 1995)
```

6. Quote from an indirect source

Use the words "as cited in" to indicate when a quotation or any information you are using from a source is itself originally from another source.

```
Lester Brown of Worldwatch believes international
agriculture production has reached its limit and that
"we're going to be in trouble on the food front before
this decade is out" (as cited in Mann, 1993, p. 51).
```

7. More than one work in a citation

As a general guideline, list two or more sources within a single parenthetical reference in the same order in which they appear on your References page. More than one work by the same author should be listed in chronological order, with the author's name mentioned once and the dates separated by commas:

```
(Thomas, 1974, 1979).
```

Works by different authors in the same parentheses are listed in alphabetical order by the author's last name, separated by semicolons:

```
(Miller, 1990; Webster & Rose, 1988).
```

8. Long quote set off from text

Start quotations of forty or more words on a new line and indent the block five spaces from the left margin. Indent the first line of the second or any subsequent paragraphs (but not the first paragraph) five additional spaces. Double-space all such quotations, omit quotation marks, and place the parenthetical citation after any end punctuation, with no period following the citation.

```
Language is everywhere. It permeates our thoughts,
mediates our relations with others, and even creeps into
our dreams. The overwhelming bulk of human knowledge is
stored and transmitted in language. Language is so
ubiquitous that we take it for granted, but without it,
society as we now know it would be impossible.

Despite its prevalence in human affairs, language is
poorly understood. (Langacker, 1968, p. 3)
```

9. Electronic source

When you cite a website, not specific information or parts of the site, it is sufficient to give the correct full name of the site and, in parentheses, its electronic address. If you are quoting, paraphrasing, or summarizing information retrieved from a website, then include an in-text citation (as you would for a print source) and a References entry. Identify the paragraph number or the section you are quoting from when the document is not paginated:.

```
(Peirce, 1869, para. 3).
```

2 Conventions for Footnotes

Footnotes are used to provide additional information that cannot be worked into the main text, information highly likely to be of interest to some readers but also likely to slow down the pace of your text or obscure your point for other readers. Therefore, even the footnotes you do choose to provide should be as brief as possible; when the information you want to add is extensive, it is better to present it in an appendix. Footnotes should be numbered consecutively, should follow the References list on a page headed "Footnotes," should be double-spaced, and should have the first line indented five spaces (or a half inch).

3 Conventions for the References Page

All works mentioned in a paper should be identified on a reference list according to the following general rules of the APA documentation system.

Format. After the final page of the paper, title a separate page "References," with no underline or quotation marks. Center the title an inch from the top of the page. Number the page in sequence with the last page of the paper.

Double-space between the title and the first entry. Set the first line flush with the left margin; the second and all subsequent lines of an entry should be indented five spaces from the left margin. This format, called a "hanging indent" format, is how a reference list looks typeset in books and journals.

Double-space both between and within entries. If your reference list exceeds one page, continue listing your references in sequence on an additional page or pages, but do not repeat the title "References."

Order of entries. Alphabetize the list of references according to authors' last names, using the first author's last name for works with multiple authors. For entries by an unknown author, alphabetize by the fist word of the title, excepting nonsignificant words (e.g., *A*, *An*, *The*).

Format for entries. The three most used general formats are described here.

GENERAL FORMAT FOR BOOKS

```
Author(s). (Year of publication). Book title. City of
    publication: Publisher.
```

GENERAL FORMAT FOR JOURNAL ARTICLES

```
Author(s). (Year of publication). Article title. Journal
    Title, volume number, inclusive page numbers.
```

GENERAL FORMAT FOR MAGAZINE AND NEWSPAPER ARTICLES

```
Author(s). (Year, month of publication). Article title.
    Publication Title, Volume, inclusive page numbers using
    the abbreviations "p." or "pp." as appropriate.
```

Authors. List the author's last name first, followed by a comma and the author's initials (not first names). When a work has more than one author, list all authors in this way, separating the names with a comma. When listing multiple authors for a single work, place an ampersand (&) before the last author's name. A period follows the author name(s).

Titles. List the complete titles and subtitles of books and articles, but capitalize only the first word of the title and any subtitle, as well as all proper nouns. Underline book titles and journal or publication titles, but do not underline article titles or place quotation marks around them. Place a period after the title.

Publishers. List publishers' names in shortened form, omitting words such as "Publishing," "Company," "Limited," and "Incorporated" (or their common abbreviations) but retail "Books" and Press." Spell out the names of university presses and organizations in full. For books, use a colon to separate the city of publication from the publisher.

Dates and page numbers. For magazines and newspapers, use commas to separate the year from the month and day, and enclose the publication dates in parentheses: (1954, May 25). Inclusive page numbers should be separated by a hyphen with no spaces: 361–375. Full sequences should be given for pages and dates: not 361–75. If pages do not follow consecutively (as in newspapers), include subsequent page numbers after a comma: pp. 1, 16. Note that "pp." precedes the page numbers for newspaper articles, but not for journal articles.

Abbreviations. State names are abbreviated, but months and country names are not. Use U.S. postal abbreviations for state abbreviations.

Following are examples of the References format for a variety of source types.

Documenting Books

1. Book by one author

```
Benjamin, J. (1988). The bonds of love: Psychoanalysis,
    feminism, and the problem of domination. New York:
    Prometheus.
```

2. Book by two or more authors

Zweigenhaft, R. L., & Domhoff, G. W. (1991). *Blacks in the White establishment*. New Haven, CT: Yale University Press.

Include the first six authors' names associated with a particular work in the References list. Shorten the number of authors by substituting "et al." for the seventh author or more. (This is a change in the Standard format established in the fifth edition of the APA Publication Manual [2001]).

3. More than one book by the same author

List two or more works by the same author (or the same author team listed in the same order) chronologically by year in the References, with the earliest first. Arrange any such works published in the same year alphabetically by title, placing lowercase letters after the dates. In either case, give full identification of author(s) for each reference listing.

Bandura, A. (1969). *Principles of behavior modification*. New York: Holt, Rinehart, and Winston.

Bandura, A. (1977a). Self-efficacy: Toward a unifying theory of behavioral change. *Psychological Review*, 84, 191–215.

Bandura, A. (1977b). *Social learning theory*. Englewood Cliffs, NJ: Prentice Hall.

If the same author is named first but listed with different coauthors, alphabetize by the last name of the second author. Works by the first author alone are listed before works with coauthors.

4. Book by a corporation, association, or organization

American Psychological Association. (2001). *Publication manual of the American Psychological Association* (5th ed.). Washington, DC: Author.

Alphabetize corporate authors by the corporate name, excluding the articles *A*, *An*, and *The*. When the corporate author is also the publisher, designate the publisher as "Author."

5. Revised edition of a book

Peek, S. (1993). *The game inventor's handbook* (Rev. ed.). Cincinnati, OH: Betterway.

6. Edited book

Schaefer, C. E., & Reid, S. E. (Eds.). (1986). *Game play: Therapeutic use of childhood games*. New York: Wiley.

Place "Ed." or "Eds.," capitalized, after the singular or plural name of the editor(s) of an edited book.

7. Book in more than one volume

Waldrep, T. (Ed.). (1985-1988). *Writers on writing* (Vols. 1-2). New York: Random House.

For a work with volumes published in different years, indicate the range of dates of publication. In citing only one volume of a multivolume work, indicate only the volume cited.

Waldrep, T. (Ed.). (1988). *Writers on writing* (Vol. 2). New York: Random House.

8. Translated or reprinted book

Freud, S. (1950). *The interpretation of dreams* (A. A. Brill, Trans.). New York: Modern Library-Random House. (Original work published 1900)

The date of the translation or reprint is in parentheses after the author's name. Indicate the original publication date parenthetically at the end of the citation, with no period. In the text, parenthetically cite the information with both dates: (Freud 1900/1950).

9. Chapter or article in an edited book

Telander, R. (1996). Senseless crimes. In C. I. Schuster & W. V. Van Pelt (Eds.), *Speculations: Readings in culture, identity, and values* (2nd ed., pp. 264-272). Upper Saddle River, NJ: Prentice Hall.

The chapter or article title is not italicized or set in quotation marks. Editors' names are listed in standard reading order (surname last). Inclusive page numbers, in parentheses, follow the title of the larger work.

10. Anonymous book

Stereotypes, distortions and omissions in U.S. history textbooks. (1977). New York: Council on Interracial Books for Children.

Do not begin an entry with "Anonymous" unless the work uses that term for its author.

11. Government document

U.S. House of Representatives, Committee on Energy and
    Commerce. (1986). Ensuring access to programming for
    the backyard satellite dish owner (Serial No. 99-127).
    Washington, DC: U.S. Government Printing Office.

For government documents, provide the higher department or governing agency only when the office or agency that created the document is not readily recognizable. If a document number is available, list it after the document title in parentheses. Write out the name of the printing agency in full, as the publisher, rather than using the abbreviation "GPO."

Documenting Periodicals

In citing periodical articles, use the same format for listing author names as for books.

12. Article in a journal paginated by volume

Hartley, J. (1991). Psychology, writing, and computers: A
    review of research. *Visible Language, 25*, 339-375.

If page numbers are continuous throughout volumes in a year, use only the volume number, italicized, following the title of the periodical.

13. Article in a journal paginated by issue

Lowther, M. A. (1977). Career change in mid-life: Its
    impact on education. *Innovator, 8*(7), 1, 9-11.

Include the issue number in parentheses if each issue of a journal is paginated separately.

14. Magazine article

Garreau, J. (1995, December). Edgier cites. *Wired, 3*,
    232-234.

For nonprofessional periodicals, include the year and month (not abbreviated) after the author's name and the volume number.

15. Newspaper article

Finn, P. (1995, September 27). Death of a U-Va. student
    raises scrutiny of off-campus drinking. *The Washington
    Post*, pp. D1, D4.

If an author is listed for the article, begin with the author's name, then list the date (spell out the month); follow with the title of the newspaper. If there is a section, combine it with the page or pages, including continued page numbers as well.

Documenting Electronic Sources

16. General Concerns and formats for documenting electronic sources

The *Publication Manual of the American Psychological Association*, fifth edition (2001) has brough the standard system for preparing manuscripts and documenting both printed and online sources fully into the computer age. The two philosophies that have always governed APA citations, however, still pertain: 1) to credit the author's work, and 2) to provide enough information for the reader to retrieve the material. In particular, when researching electronic sources, consider carefully the accessibility of the source in deciding to use it in your paper, asking whether the source is widely available or limited to your campus, and whether the material is likely to remain on the electronic path or be archived to tape. If the source is available in the same format both in a nonelectronic (print) and an electronic form, it is preferable to document the nonelectronic format rather than the electronic one.

Formats for documenting electronic media have been changing and will continue to evolve. The 2001 APA *Publication Manual* (5th edition; see pp. 268–281 especially) and the APA Web page for electronic document citations (http://www. apastyle.org/elecref.html) are the best sources for up-to-date advice on standard models. The newest APA style recommendations divide electronic sources between two large categories: (1) sources on the Internet, divided into two types—periodicals (sources published regularly, such as journals, newsletters, magazines, etc.) and nonperiodicals (books, stand-alone documents, reports, brochures, audiovisual media, etc.); and (2) other electronic sources (CD-ROMs, databases, electronic mail, etc.).

The retrieval statement is a key feature of electronic source references. APA guidelines call for accurate and current electronic addresses (URLs) and correct names for host sites or databases in the retrieval statement. The retrieval date gives a reader infomration on when the site was available to you. Several models are provided below that show the correct use of the retrieval statement.

The APA recommends using the models for print periodicals when documenting online articles that do not vary from their printed versions. In such cases, add [Electronic version] after the title and before the period to complete the citation. When the electronic format alters the printed version (e.g., no pagination, added data or links), then cite as an online document, using a retrieval statement and the name of the database and/or the URL. APA guidelines ask for the identification of the server or the website in a retrieval statement only when it would be helpful in finding the source; for example, it is not necessary to state "Retrieved from the World Wide Web" since it is the most common access point to the Internet.

Cautionary Note: Sources you uncover on the Internet may or may not contain valid information. Check the credentials of the site (the author, the publisher, whether the content conforms to information you have found in other sources) before you decide to use it in your paper. Ultimately, you are responsible for the accuracy and value of the information you rely on in your writing. As the computer people are fond of saying, "Garbage in, garbage out (the GIGO principle)."

17. Online journal articles unaltered from the print version

Green, C. D. (1992) Of immortal mythological beasts:
   Operationism in psychology [Electronic version]. *Theory
   and Psychology*, 2, 291–320.

Many online articles are provided unchanged from the print version (e.g., original page numbers are indicated, no data or links have been added, etc.), then cite the same as you would the print text. However, add *[Electronic version]* after the title to complete the citation.

When the source has been altered from its print version in any way (making the online version to that extent unique), then add a retrieval statement and the URL to complete the citation. If your source is an Internet-only periodical or if you retrieved the article via file transfer protocol (ftp), you would follow the same format, as in model 18 below.

18. Abstract from aggregated database

Current APA guidelines indicate that when citing a source from an aggregated database as a reference, follow the format appropriate to the work retrieved, but add a statement that gives the date of retrieval and the name of the database. For example:

Electronic copy of a journal article retrieved from database:

Carpenter, Joni. (1993). Speaking, writing and knowing as a
   woman: Making space for difference in the composition
   classroom. *Community Review*, 13, 8–13. Abstract
   retrieved May 4, 2002, from Ebsco Host database.

19. Online article with altered format or content

Kapadia, S. (1995, November). A tribute to Mahatma Gandhi:
   His views on women and social exchange [19 paragraphs].
   Journal of South Asia Women's Studies, 1 (1). Retrieved
   October 21, 1998, from http://www.shore.net/
   ~india/jsaws/

For online journal articles, indicate the number of paragraphs in brackets after the title of the article. The issue number follows the volume number, in parentheses. Give the access date in the "Retrieved . . ." statement, as well as the URL, with no end punctuation.

Usually, you do not need to include a descriptor for an article from an online journal. In the following example, notice the description in square brackets following the title, volume number, and page number. It is added when it helps a reader retrieve the source. (Most descriptors of documents follow the title; for example, to identify a brochure or motion picture.)

Lewis, R. (1995, December 24). Chronobiology researchers say their field's time has come. *The Scientist*, 9, p. 14 [Online newspaper]. Retrieved December 30, 1997, from http://www.the-cientist.library.upenn.edu/yr1995/dec/chrono_951211.html

The following example is for an article provided on the website of the Knowledge Science Institute of the University of Calgary; the URL is necessary because the format of the article is not the same as the print version, and a reader should be able to locate the same source without difficulty.

Shaw, M. L. G., & Gaines, B. R. (1992, October). Kelly's "geometry psychological space" and its significance for cognitive modeling. *The New Psychologist*, 23-31. Retrieved March 8, 2002, from http://ksi.cpsc.ucalgary.ca/articles/NewPsych92/

Nonperiodicals

20. Online document published by a private organization or group

American Psychiatric Association. (2001). *Coping with a national tragedy-Resources, Tools, and Other Links.* September 20, 2001. Retrieved January 6, 2002, from http://psych.org/public_info/copydisaster92001.cfm

If the document has no revision or publication date, insert the abbreviation *(n.d.)* after the title and before the retrieval statement.

21. Document available on a university or project website

Peirce, C. S. (1869, November 25). The English doctrine of
    ideas. *Nation 9*, 461–462. Retrieved January 16, 2002,
    from IUPUI (Indiana University and Purdue University,
    Indianapolis) Peirce Edition Project website:
    http://www.iupui.edu/%7Epeirce/web/writings/v2/w2/w2_30/
    v2_30.htm

This example was retrieved from a website for the Peirce Edition Project (dedicated to the works of philosopher Charles Sander Peirce), a large university project. The URL allows the reader to reach the cited article directly, without navigating the complex site. An online book, report, or data survey can be cited using this model or model 24.

22. Abstract retrieved online from a university site

Bar-Tal, Y., Kishnon-Rabin, L., & Tabak, N. (in press). The
    effect of need and ability to achieve cognitive
    structuring on cignitive structuring). *Journal of
    Personality and Social Psychology*. Abstract retrieved
    March 7, 2002, from Purdue University, Social Cognition
    Paper Archive and Information Center database:
    http://www/psych.purdue.edu/~esmith/bt.html

23. Electronic mail message

Electronic mail is considered a personal communication, not available to your readers. Cite it within your text, as you would any other personal information sorce (interview, letter, etc.).

Wilson reported that his data did not match Baer's
conclusions (K. T. Wilson, personal communication,
December 12, 2001).

24. Newsgroup, electronic mailing list, or discussion group posting

Trehub, A. (2002, January 28). The conscious access
    hypothesis [Msg. 18]. Message posted to University
    of Houston Psyche Discussion Forum:
    http://listserv.uh.edu/cgi-bin/
    wa?A2=ind0201&L=psyche-b&F=&S=&P=2334

Other Electronic Sources

25. Aggregated databases

A searchable, "aggregated database" is a selected group of resources stored in an electronic form for simplified, focused electronic access. You are not required to document how you accessed the database—via portable CD-ROM, on a library server, via a supplier World Wide Web site—but a retrieval statement that correctly names the source (in this case, the database) and gives the data of retrieval is always necessary. (If you include an item or accession number, place it in parentheses after the title of your document.) Give the URL only when the information will help your reader locate the specific material. Do not italicize the names of databases.

Freud, S. (1913). *Interpretation of dreams* (A. A. Brill, Trans.). New York: Macmillan. Retrieved March 1, 2002, from Classics in the History of Psychology database.

This online book can be obtained on the Internet. A title or author keyword serarch will obtain the document in the database. If the database were obtained on CD-ROM or a library server, the citation would be the same.

26. Electronic copy of an article, abstract, or data file

Harnad, S. (1992). Other bodies, other minds: A machine incarnation of an old philosophical problems. *Minds and Machines 1*, 43-54. Retrieved February 25, 2002, from Cognitive Science at Southhampton E-Print Archive database: http://cogsci.soton.ac.uk/~harnad/genpub.html

27. Computer software, program, or language

Commonly used commercial computer software and programming languages (Microsoft Word 5.1, e.g.) do not require a References page entry. Identify the correct name of the software, program, or langauge along with the version number in your text. If the software is not widely distributed or unfamiliar, cite according to this model.

HyperCard (Version 2.2) [Computer software]. (1993). Cupertino, CA: Apple Computer.

28. Motion picture, audio recording, and other nonprint media

Curtiz, M. (Director). (1942). *Casablanca* [Motion picture].
   United States: Warner Bros.

    Alphabetize a motion picture listing by the name of the person or persons with primary responsibility for the product. Identify the medium in brackets following the title, and indicate both country location and name of the distributor (as publisher). Other identifying information should appear in parentheses.

Sample pages using APA documentation system

The most recent breakthrough in breast cancer research has discovered a gene called BRCA1 that has been linked to breast cancer through heredity. A woman increases her lifetime risk of developing breast cancer by 85% if she has the BRCA1 gene, and she will usually develop cancer at a younger age (American Cancer Society, 1997). Some women diagnosed with the gene feel that the risks are too great and choose, consequently, to have a preventative mastectomy (the complete removal of the breast). Laversen and Stukane (1996) indicate that since research is underway to develop a drug which will treat the mutation on the BRCA1 gene many women in the future will not have to resort to such invasive techniques.

But even if a woman does not have any of the known risk factors for breast cancer, she may not be out of danger. The National Institutes of Health reveal that most women who develop breast cancer have never had a family history of the disease, nor do they fall into any of the other high-risk categories (1997).

Women are therefore urged to undergo yearly mammograms once they reach the age of 40, and earlier if they suspect they may be at risk. A mammogram uses low-dose radiation to take an x-ray of the breast. In the 1990s mammograms use as little as 1/40 of the radiation of the 1960s and therefore are considered safe (Cancer Information Service, personal communication,

*Note: APA papers should be double spaced throughout. For space, this example is single spaced.

March 21, 1997). But mammograms are not fool-
proof: Radiologists estimate that 10-15% of can-
cers may be missed (American Association of
Retired Persons [AARP], 1991).

References

American Association of Retired Persons [AARP].
     (1991). *Chances are you need a mammogram: A
     Guide for midlife and older women*
     [Brochure]. Washington, DC: Author.
American Cancer Society. (1997). *Cancer facts &
     figures 1997* [Home page]. Retrieved October
     20, 1998 from the World Wide Web:
     http://www.cancer.org/abacs.html
Laversen, N. H., & Stukane, E. (1996). *The com-
     plete book of breast care*. New York: Bal-
     lantyne Books.
National Institutes of Health. (1997, January
     21-23). *NIH consensus statement* [Press
     release]. Retrieved October 20, 1998, from
     http://www.odp.od.nih.gov/consensus/
     statements/cic/103/103_stmt.html

HEADING CENTERED   "1"

References

Allen, F. E. (1991, March 10). Great Lakes
    cleanup enlists big volunteers. *The Wall
    Street Journal*, p. B1.

Carlson, L., Grove, S. J., & Kangun, N.
    (1993). A content analysis of
    environmental advertising claims: a
    matrix methods approach. *Journal of
    Advertising, 22*(9), 27-39.

Decker, C., and Stammer, L. (1989, March 4).
    Bush asks ban on CFC to save ozone. *Los
    Angeles Times*, p. A1.

Do people allow themselves to be that
    gullible? (1994, September). *Earth
    First! 9*, 6. Don't you wish we could
    just do this to CFC's natural gas
    advertisement. (1994, December 7).
    Audubon, 12, 7.

The ecology channel (1996). [On-line].
    Available http:/www.ecology.com/

Fogel, B. (1985). *Energy: choices for the
    future*. New York: Franklin Watts.

From this day onward I will restore the earth
    where I am. (1994, November-December).
    [Chevrolet advertisement]. *Audubon,
    11-12*, 18-19.

Kennedy, D., & Grumbly, T.P. (1988).
    Automotive emissions research. In A.
    Watson, R. R. Bates, & D. Kennedy
    (Eds.), *Air pollution, the automobile,
    and public health* (pp. 3-9). Cambridge,
    MA: National Academy Press.

Margin annotations:

AUTHORS
ARE LISTED
ALPHA-
BETICALLY.

INITIALS ARE
USED FOR
FIRST AND
MIDDLE
NAMES.

DATE
FOLLOWS
AUTHOR
OR TITLE,
(NO
AUTHOR IS
IDENTIFIED)

INDENTED
5 SPACES

"P." OR "PP."
IS USED FOR
PAGE
NUMBERS IN
BOOKS OR
POPULAR
PERIODICALS.

DOUBLE-
SPACED

ONLY FIRST
WORD AND
PROPER
NAMES ARE
CAPITALIZED
IN ARTICLE
TITLE.

"P." OR "PP."
IS NOT USED
TO INDICATE
PAGES IN A
PROFESSIONAL
JOURNAL.

BOOK AND
PERIODICAL
TITLES ARE
ITALICIZED.

5

Documenting Sources:
CSE Systems

The sciences (biology, botany, zoology, anatomy, physiology, chemistry, and physics) all follow, with slight variations and modifications, the style of the Council of Science Editors' (CSE) format. If you are writing a paper in the sciences, check with your instructor or journal editor for the preferred conventions and modifications for the particular discipline.

The *Scientific Style and Format: CBE Manual for Authors, Editors, and Publishers* (6th ed.) recognizes two different systems for citing and documenting sources: the citation-sequence system and the name-year system. These two systems are widely used in scientific papers. (Note: The Council of Science Editors was formerly known as the Council of Biology Editors. Thus, the title of their most recent publication is still the *CBE Manual.*)

1 Conventions for the Citation-Sequence System When Citing Sources In-Text

Superscript numbers are used in the body of the paper to identify and designate entries on the references page. Entries on the references page are listed according to the order in which they appear in the body of the paper, not in alphabetical order, and every citation to an entry uses the same number, i.e., the first citation is given the superscript number 1 throughout the paper. The CSE acknowledges that some editors prefer the use of parentheses for the number and placement on the line instead of above it. Multiple source citations are handled by separating each superscript number with commas.

```
"has been shown1 to replace beta inhibitors. . . ."

"have been shown1,6,14 to replace beta inhibitors. . . ."
```

2 Conventions for the Name-Year System When Citing Sources In-Text

The author's name and the year of publication are given in parentheses following the materials being cited, and the entries on the references page are alphabetized according to the last name of the author (or whatever element is used to begin the entry). The author's name and year are not separated by a comma (Author date, not Author, date).

> "has been shown (Jones 1998) to replace beta
> inhibitors. . . ."

> "have been shown (Jones and Johnson 1998) to replace
> beta inhibitors. . . ."

Note that multiple authors in a citation require an "and" instead of an ampersand (&). If the source has three or more authors, the first author's name is given followed by "and others."

Multiple citations that occur at one point in the paper are listed with a single set of parentheses and given in chronological sequence from earliest to latest (Jones 1996; Anderson 1997; Smith 1998). If two authors published in the same year, they are listed alphabetically by the authors' names.

Unreferenced citations, such as personal communications and oral presentations at conventions, are described in-text, usually within parentheses:

> "have been shown (in a panel discussion by John Jones
> and Albert Betterthwaite at the September 1998 meeting
> of the National Mathematical Convention, Albany, New
> York; unreferenced) to replace beta inhibitors. . . ."

3 Conventions for Both Systems on the References Page

General Principles

1. No comma separates the author(s) name(s) and initial(s).
2. No periods separate the initials.
3. Major elements in the entry are separated by periods.
4. The semicolon is used to separate items not directly related.
5. The colon indicates that what follows is subordinate, such as a subtitle and page numbers following a volume number.
6. Titles are not italicized, underlined, boldfaced, or placed in quotation marks. Position indicates what is an article title and what is a journal title. Single-word titles are given in full; multiple-word titles may be abbreviated if clear (Int J Epidemiol for International Journal of Epidemiology).
7. An anonymous author is designated by [Anonymous].
8. Identifiers are placed in brackets immediately after the title (New age politics [editorial]).
9. Article titles capitalize only the first letter of the first word and any proper nouns or adjectives. The word which follows the colon (as in a subtitle) is not capitalized unless a proper noun or adjective. Capitalized abbreviations (IBM) and symbols (pH) are exceptions.

Book

C-S: Author(s) [or editor(s)]. Title. Place of publication: publisher name; Year. Number of pages.

```
1. Smith D. Zoology. New York: J Wiley; 1998. 1256 p.
```

N-Y: Author(s) [or editor(s)]. Year. Title. Place of publication: publisher name. Number of pages.

```
Smith D. 1998. Zoology. New York: J Wiley. 1256 p.
```

Journal

C-S: Author(s). Article title. Journal title year month;volume number(issue number):inclusive pages.

```
1. Baslehoff Q. Polynominals. Science 1993 Oct
   14;112(10):234-39.
```

N-Y: Author(s), Year. Article title. Journal title volume number(issue number):inclusive pages.

```
Baslehoff Q. 1993. Polynominals. Science 112(10):234-39.
```

Newspapers

C-S: Author(s). Article title. Newspaper title and date of publication;section designator:page number(column number)

```
4. Spectrol B. CFCs and the environment. Denver Post 1997
   Aug 21;Sect B:6(col 2).
```

N-Y: Author(s). Date of publication. Article title. Newspaper title;section designator:page number(column number).

```
Spectrol B. 1997 Aug 21. CFCs and the environment. Denver
   Post;Sect B:6(col 2).
```

Magazines

C-S: Author(s). Article title. Magazine title and date of publication:page numbers.

```
4. Johansson C. HIV outbreaks in Atlanta. Scientific
   American 1991:115-25.
```

N-Y: Author(s). Date of publication. Article title. Magazine title:page numbers.

```
Johansson C. 1991. HIV outbreaks in Atlanta. Scientific
   American:115-25.
```

Electronic publications

The CSE follows the format adopted by the National Library of Medicine (NLM), distinguishing between sources that are transportable (computer disks, for example) and sources that are available through telecommunication (online sources). Most electronic sources in literature written on science subjects are journal articles. If a book or other non-periodical source is being referenced, include the pertinent data according to the CSE system, add sufficient information for identification of the source as electronic, and provide information for retrieval.

Some electronic journals do not indicate volume, issue, and page numbers. In these cases, the critical data are the article's date of publication and a designator (access date or document number). Many varieties of format have been and are being used, making easy conformity to samples sometimes difficult. The general rule to follow is that "more" is preferable: if in doubt, provide additional information to that listed in the samples below, such as version numbers, number of lines or paragraphs, number of disks, size of disks (5 1/4 or 3 1/2), system requirements, user's manual availability, and the like.

Journal articles

C-S: Author(s). Title of article. Abbreviated journal title [type of medium] date of publication;volume number(issue number):pagination. Availability statement. Date accessed, if needed.

```
16. Smith R. Neonomials in plasma. J Math Soc [serial
    online] 1995;1(3):34-45. Available from: Public Access
    Computer System Forum PACS via the INTERNET. Accessed
    1998 Apr 30.
```

N-Y: Author(s). Date of publication. Title of article. Abbreviated journal title [type of medium]; volume number (issue number): pagination. Availability statement. Date accessed, if needed.

```
Smith R. 1995. Neonomials in plasma. J Math Soc [serial
    online];1(3):34-45. Available from: Public Access
    Computer Systems Forum PACS via the INTERNET. Accessed
    1998 Apr 30.
```

Surveying Procedures and Techniques

GPS equipment provides a surveyor with several methods of locating points on the earth's surface. Each of these procedures and techniques have varying degrees of accuracy and time requirements. A surveyor must determine what accuracy level is required for a particular project, then use the proper method to obtain the predetermined criteria. A surveyor can obtain various results by increasing the amount of GPS receivers and providing a longer satellite observation time.[1]

A static survey is a method of GPS technology that produces positional information to the centimeter level of accuracy. A static survey is accomplished by occupying a point of known coordinates, and using this information to help refine the location of other points. The GPS receiver occupying the point of known coordinates can compare and adjust any discrepancies of the data received from satellites. With these small adjustment factors calculated, the receiver can accurately locate additional points occupied by other receivers.[10]

Traditional static is the technique of GPS positioning in which one base receiver is placed over a point of known coordinates (longitude, latitude, and elevation) while others are placed over new permanent stations to be positioned. Observation time is usually one hour or more depending on the receiver, the satellites' geometric configuration, the length of line, and atmospheric conditions. This technique is used for long lines in geodetic control, photogrammetric control for aerial surveys, and precise engineering surveys. Traditional static surveys are used as a fall-back technique when the available geometric array of satellites is not compatible with other GPS techniques used for surveying.[2,8]

RapiRapid static is a technique developed in the early 1990s. It provides identical results to the traditional static method, but uses a much shorter observation time. Typically, for distances less than 10 kilometers, a 15 minute period of observation time is sufficient. The exact amount of recording time is determined from a wide range of factors, including the number of visible satellites, the geometric strength of the satellite constellation. . . .[4]

References

1. Ferguson J. What is it we obtain from GPS? J. Prof. Surveying 1993 July-Aug.;17(4);3-4.

2. Livingston M. GPS: The surveyor's hi-tech tool. Point of Beginning 1993, February-March;15(2);34, 39.

3. Advanstar Publications. GPS world showcase [Brochure]. Eugene, OR; Author. 4 p.

4. Diltea S. Real men don't ask directions. Popular Science [serial on-line] 1995;246(3):86-89, 120-121 Available from: Wilson Indexes, WSCI Database. [Accessed 1995 Apr 30].

5. Kavanagh BF, Bird SJG. Surveying principles and applications (4th ed.). Englewood Cliffs, NJ: Prentice Hall; 1996. 459 p.

6. Ferguson J. The state of GPS in 1995. Professional Surveyor 1995 July-Aug;15(7);6-10.

7. Allen Precision Equipment. Hot 1995 summer specials [Brochure]. Atlanta: Author; 1995. 12 p.

8. Harrison N. Full strength GPS. Professional Surveyor 1995 July-Aug;15(7);14-15.

9. McCormac JC. Surveying (3rd ed.). Englewood Cliffs, NJ: Prentice Hall; 1995. 791 p.

10. Trimble Navigation. Ensign GPS & EnsignXL GPS: Hand-held GPS systems. Austin: Univ. of Texas Press; 1995. 652 p.